C000126726

UNCAPTURED CRETE

Diana Conyers

© Mystis Editions, A. Tsintaris & Co.
Iraklio, Crete, Greece
71500, 108 Men.Parlama str.,
Estavromenos, t.: 0030 2810 346451
www.mystis.gr
info@mystis.gr

ISBN: 978-618-5024-50-5

Cover Design - Layout: Mystis Editions, based on a photograph by
Fiona Wilson.

for Ashley
who unfortunately never made it to Crete

CONTENTS

LIST OF PHOTOGRAPHS

Map of Crete

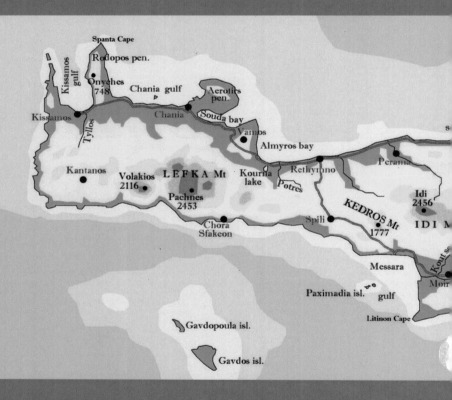

Spanta Cape

Rodopos pen.

Kissamos gulf

Onyches
748

Chania gulf

Aerotirs
pen.

Kissamos

Chania

Souda bay

Tyllos

Vamos

Almyros bay

Kantanos

Volakios
2116

L E F K A Mt

Pachnes
2453

Kourna
lake

Potres

Rethymno

Perama

Idi
2456

KEDROS Mt

I D I M

Chora
Sfakeon

Spili

1777

Messara

Mon

Paximadia isl.

gulf

Litinon Cape

Gavdopoula isl.

Gavdos isl.

Greece

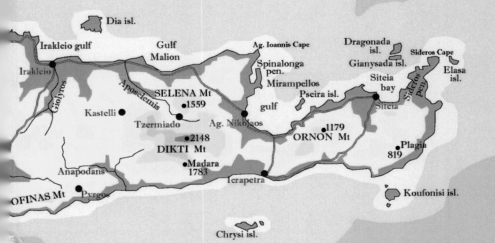

Dia isl.

Irakleio gulf

Irakleio

Giolyros

Aposelemis

Kastelli

Gulf
Malion

SELENA Mt
●1559

Tzermiado

Ag. Ioannis Cape

Spinalonga
pen.

Mirampellos

gulf

Ag. Nikolaos

Dragonada
isl.

Gianysada isl.

Siteia
bay

Pseira isl.

Siteros Cape

Elasa
isl.

Siteros pen.

Siteia

●2148
DIKTI Mt

●Madara
1783

Anapodaris

OFINAS Mt   ●Pyrgos

Ierapetra

ORNON Mt
●1179

●Plagia
819

Koufonisi isl.

Chrysi isl.

Acknowledgements

Many people have contributed to the production of this book. My biggest debt is to Fiona Wilson, who helped me to formulate the topic and to interpret many aspects of Cretan history and society. During our travels together, both in Crete and on the Greek mainland, the book triggered many fascinating discussions. She also painstakingly read and commented on two drafts and encouraged me to publish it. Without her inspiration and support, there would be no book – or at least, not this book.

Three other people also played an important role. The first is my long-suffering Greek teacher, Manolis Petarsis, who not only tried to teach me Greek but also advised me on many aspects of Cretan politics and society. It is my fault, not his, that I have not made more progress in learning Greek. The second is Peter Rogers, who shared his knowledge of the history of Crete, advised me on historical sources and read a draft of the history chapter. The third is Maria Kontou, who gave me a brief but very solid grounding in the Greek language before I moved to Crete and later visited the island and shared her impressions of it with me.

Several other people read and commented on drafts of the book. I would like in particular to thank Amanda Bidirini for reading the final draft. Her comments were both insightful and encouraging. Thanks also to Will French and Jackie Sefton, both of whom read early drafts, and to my sister Bridget Kindler, who read the final draft and (not for the first time) served as my proof reader.

On the production side, I am very grateful to Mystis Edtions for publishing the book. I am pleased that it is being published in Crete by a local publisher. I would also like to thank Rob Mellors for taking the photograph of Spinalonga for me, Maurice Sheppard for editing the last photograph, the Skoulas family for allowing me to include a picture of their coffee shop (the *Kafeneio Michalos Skoulas*) in Anogeia, and Stella Charina and Yannis Metsagkourakis for permitting me to include a photo of them performing in Myrtos.

Finally, I would like to thank all the people whom I have met in Crete and who have enriched my life here. Many of you are mentioned in the book and, although in most cases I have used pseudonyms, I am sure you will recognise yourselves. I hope I have not offended anyone! Needless to say, any errors of fact or interpretation are entirely my own responsibility.

Aghios Nikolaos, Crete
June 2015

INTRODUCTION

Chapter 1

Uncaptured Crete: The Birth of an Idea

At daybreak I awoke, and there, to our right, lay the proud,
wild and lordly island. The pale-pink mountains were
smiling through the mists beneath the autumnal sun. Round
our ship, the indigo-blue sea was still seething restlessly.

'How beautiful Crete is', he murmured, 'how beautiful! Ah!
If only I were an eagle, to admire the whole of Crete from
an airy height!'

(Nikos Kazantzakis, *Zorba the Greek*, London, Faber and
Faber, 1961, p.21; and *Freedom and Death*, London, Faber and
Faber, 1966, p.65.)

Crete has a powerful effect on anyone who visits it. This is reflected in much of the literature by travellers to the island. Michael
Llewellyn Smith, who was there in the 1960s, wrote that there is
something about Crete that 'draws like a magnet'.[1] This magnetic
attraction is also reflected in the writings of Cretans themselves.
The obvious example is Nikos Kazantzakis, the island's most famous author. Kazantzakis travelled widely throughout his life,
but his attachment to his birthplace remained strong. He wrote
two novels set in Crete: *Captain Michalis* (published in English as

3

Freedom and Death) and, probably his best known work, *Zorba the Greek*. His feelings about the island are, as the above quotations indicate, vividly portrayed in these works.

My first visit to Crete was in September 2006. It happened more or less by chance. My husband and I were then living in the UK and we were looking for a cheap autumn holiday in a warm place. We knew very little about Crete, but it seemed the obvious choice. However, during that first visit we were captured by Crete's spell. We returned three years in succession, staying in different places each time, and on the third visit we decided to move there. My husband had been retired for many years and I was ready to do so. In January 2010 we bought an apartment on the outskirts of Aghios Nikolaos, a picturesque port and tourist resort on the northeast coast.

The Greeks have a proverb that says that 'when man makes plans, God laughs', and unfortunately that proved true in our case. Soon after we bought the apartment, my husband suffered a major stroke and so spent the last years of his life in hospitals and nursing homes in the UK instead of in Crete. However, after his death in 2012, I decided to go ahead with our original plan. I still had the Cretan apartment and felt in need of a change. I sold my UK flat, retired from my job and, in April 2013, finally moved to Aghios Nikolaos.

During my first year there, I began to reflect on Crete and, in particular, my reactions to it. These reactions were mainly positive. Crete was one of the most beautiful and interesting places I had ever visited. I loved the scenery, especially the juxtaposition of sea and mountains, and the long hot summers, and I was fascinated by the history and culture. These were the things that had brought me and my husband back to Crete year after year and had eventually led me to come and live there. However, there was also something about Crete that sometimes made me feel slightly uneasy. There were times when I felt overpowered by the physical environment and, although in many respects I felt

4

really at home, I was also very much aware of being an 'outsider'.

I knew that my unease was due in large part to my personal situation. I had spent most of my working life outside the UK and so was used to living in new places and being an 'outsider'. But this time was different. I had not come to Crete to work, but to retire. I lacked the security and purpose of a job and there was an element of permanence that I had not had to face before. However, I had a feeling that my reactions also reflected something about Crete itself. Therefore, in April 2014, a year after my move, I decided to write about my experiences and observations. I enjoy writing and have always used it as a means of coming to terms with my personal situation. In this case, I thought it would be a good way of understanding more about Crete as well as about my own feelings.

Six months later, I found that I had written nearly 50,000 words. I had written about all sorts of things, from the landscape, history and culture to the economic and political problems and the impenetrable bureaucracy. Curiosity had led me not only to relate my own experiences but also to do some documentary research, particularly into the history, language and politics. I had also found myself making comparisons with other places where I had lived and worked, especially Africa, which was my husband's home for most of his life and mine for nearly twenty years.

More importantly, however, I had begun to realise that both the character of the island and my own reactions to it could be understood in terms of its geography and history, and I had begun to formulate a theory to explain why this was so. The basis of my theory is that, today as in the past, Crete has the power not only to attract outsiders, but also to repel them. I will explain what I mean in detail in subsequent chapters, but briefly my argument is as follows. Because of its resources and strategic location, the island's history has been one of successive invasions and occupations – by mainland Greeks, Romans, Venetians, Arabs, Turks and (during the Second World War) Germans and Italians. However, due to the sometimes hostile physical environment and the resilience of the Cretan people, these invaders found it difficult to penetrate and thus control the whole island and were never able to subjugate the local population. Over the centuries, the Cretans developed the capacity to take what they wanted from the invaders and ignore what was of no benefit to them, to tolerate them if they did not cause too much trouble and to revolt against them if they did. Many of the outsiders were gradually absorbed into the local society, but on Cretan terms.

So far, my theory was not original; many other observers have drawn similar conclusions. However, my analysis led me to two further insights. First, I was reminded of a book I once read about Tanzania, written by a well-known Swedish political scientist, Goran Hyden. The book was called *Beyond Ujamaa in Tanzania: Underdevelopment and an Uncaptured Peasantry*.[2] In the book, Hyden tried to explain why the Tanzanian Government's *ujamaa* village policy, which had attempted to reorganise the country's rural population into communal settlements, had had little success. His argument was that the rural people had become resilient to such efforts. They had managed to maintain their identity and way of life despite many changes in government, including two periods of colonial rule (German and British) and the early, pre-*ujamaa* years of independence. *Ujamaa* was merely the latest challenge. He coined the term 'uncaptured' to describe their resilience. It is a concept that I have found very useful in explaining how and why people have survived periods of hardship in other parts of Africa, and I was reminded of it again here in Crete. It struck me that the Cretans are an uncaptured people.

The second insight emerged during discussions with a friend, to whom I showed the first draft of what I had written. I realised that Crete is currently in the midst of another invasion. This invasion stems from the forces of globalisation and Crete's membership (as part of Greece) of the European Union. It is manifested in a massive influx of people and capital, through tourism and other forms of trade and investment, and in the increasing influence of regional and global institutions of governance. Moreover, I realised that I am part of that invasion and that in my daily life I am observing and experiencing the way in which Crete is responding to it.

This book has two objectives. The first is to explain the above argument in more detail, and in particular to demonstrate how what is happening in Crete today is in many respects just another phase in its long history of invasion and resistance. The second is to give existing and prospective visitors, including tourists and long-term residents, some idea of what the island is like, including not just its geography and history, its language, religion and culture, and its economy and politics, but also the reasons for its magnetic attraction.

The rest of the book is divided into six chapters. Chapters 2 and 3 provide the geographical and historical background. Chapter 2 describes Crete's strategic position and its spectacular but in many respects harsh physical environment, which both attracts and repels outsiders. Chapter 3 provides an overview of its history, focusing on the successive waves of invasion and the Cretans' response to them. Then I turn to the present situation and what I call the latest invasion. Chapter 4 describes the various forms that this invasion is taking, including the extent and impact of tourism, other forms of foreign investment and trade, the large influxes of migrant labour and people who, like me, have chosen to retire to the island, and the impact of the institutions of European and global governance.

The next two chapters discuss the implications of this invasion. Chapter 5 looks at the Cretan response. It argues that the Cretans are, once again, trying to get as much as they can from the situation while retaining their own identity and independence. Chapter 6 then considers the outsider's perspective. It maintains that a complex combination of physical, linguistic, cultural and bureaucratic barriers make it difficult for outsiders to penetrate all aspects of the island and, in particular, to become fully integrated into the local society. As in the past, integration is possible, but it takes time and is on Cretan terms. Finally, in Chapter 7, I look briefly at what the future holds – for Crete and for me. I consider how long Crete will be able to remain 'uncaptured' and how my analysis of the situation has affected my own approach to life in Crete.

Before embarking on this journey of exploration and explanation, I should say something about my approach. Firstly, I should explain that, although I have been referring to the people of Crete as if they were a homogeneous group, that is not of course the case. The island has, from the earliest times, been populated by many different peoples. That is part of the story that I will tell. However, there is also a sense of common identity that binds people together and thus justifies certain generalisations.

Secondly, for most of its history, Crete has had strong links with mainland Greece and for the last century it has been an integral part of the Greek state. Consequently, many of the characteristics of Crete that I will describe apply also to Greece as a whole. This is also part of the story. I will, as and when necessary, indicate when I am referring to the entire country rather than specifically to Crete and I will look at Crete's evolving relationship with Greece.

Thirdly, Crete is obviously not the only part of the world with a history of successive invasions and occupations, nor the only place where people have adapted to them in this way. Although I will make such comparisons from time to time, my aim here is not to develop a comprehensive theory, but simply to tell the story of Crete. It is an interesting case study in its own right – and it is the place where I happened to be when embarking on this venture.

Finally, I should make a few comments about the sources of my data. I have, as I mentioned earlier, done a considerable amount of research and will use secondary sources where appropriate, particularly in Chapters 2 and 3. However, my main source of information is my own observations and experiences. I hope that this will not only make the book more interesting but also give readers some idea of what life is actually like for an outsider in Crete and, perhaps most important of all, convey something of the spirit of Crete that makes it such a fascinating place to visit.

PART ONE
BACKGROUND

Chapter 2

Geography: A Land that Attracts and Repels

> We thought Crete the most beautiful island in the
> world: a miniature continent with its Alps, its deserts
> and jungles, its arctic and its tropics, its Wales and
> Morocco and China, crammed into an area hardly
> bigger than Long Island (New York) or Devon plus
> Cornwall. (Rackham, O. and J. Moody, *The Making of
> the Cretan Landscape*, Manchester University Press, 1996,
> p.xi)

Crete's physical environment has had a major impact on its social, economic and political history and it continues to play a significant role today. In this chapter, I will provide a brief overview of this environment, including the island's location, its landscape, the climate, and the flora and fauna. In so doing, I hope also to convey something of the beauty of Crete to which Rackham and Moody refer in the quotation above. I will draw heavily on their book, *The Making of the Cretan Landscape,* which is probably the best source of information on the subject in English – and also a beautifully written book.

Location

> If you looked at a map of the world and knew no history, you could guess from her position that foreigners would covet this lovely island, and indeed they have. (Llewellyn Smith, M., *Crete: The Great Island*, Longman, 1965; online edition 2007, p.12).

There are three major features of Crete's location. First, it is an island. This has affected not only its communication with the rest of the world but also other aspects of its physical environment. Second, it is located in a strategic position at the eastern end of the Mediterranean. In the past, its position put it at a critical point on the shipping routes between the western Mediterranean and Constantinople (or Istanbul, as it is now called nearly everywhere except in Greece). Third, it is located on the periphery not only of Greece but also of Europe. It is the point where three continents – Europe, Asia and Africa – meet. The eastern tip of the island is nearer to Turkey than to Athens and the south-western tip is as near to the Libyan coast as it is to Athens.

We shall see in Chapter 3 how these three factors have had a major impact on the island's history. And in Chapters 4 and 5 we will see that, although advances in communication (such as the development of air travel and telecommunications) have reduced their importance, they continue to play a significant role today. In fact, they even influenced my initial decision to come to Crete. I assumed that, since it was the southern-most place in Europe, it would also be the warmest – an assumption that, as we shall see later, proved to be only partially correct.

Landscape

> This Cretan countryside resembled good prose, carefully ordered, sober, free from superfluous ornament, powerful and restrained. … It said what it had to say with a manly austerity. But between

the severe lines one could discern an unexpected
sensitiveness and tenderness; in the sheltered hollows,
the lemon and orange trees perfumed the air, and
from the vastness of the sea emanated an inexhaustible
poetry. (Nikos Kazantzakis, *Zorba the Greek,* Faber and
Faber 1961, p.34)

Crete is the largest of the Greek islands. However, it is relatively
small by international standards. In area, it is about 8,300 square
kilometres, which - as Rackham and Moody point out - is not
much bigger than Long Island, New York. In shape, it is long and
narrow. It is about 225 kilometres long, while its width varies
from about 55 kilometres at the widest point to 12 kilometres at
the narrowest. The narrowest point is not far from Aghios Nikolaos, the town where I live. Aghios Nikolaos is on the north coast,
but a 30-minute drive takes one to Ierapetra, the main town on
the south coast.

I find it relatively easy to remember Crete's dimensions because it
is very similar in size and shape to Lake Kariba, a large reservoir
on Africa's Zambezi River, which constitutes the border between
Zimbabwe and Zambia. My husband (who was Zimbabwean)
and I lived on the shores of Lake Kariba for nine years - first at
the eastern end, near the dam wall, and later at the western end.
Kariba, like Crete, is an incredibly beautiful area. The big difference, of course, is that Crete is an island, while Kariba is a lake.
In other words, Crete is like an inverted version of Lake Kariba.

The two most notable features of Crete's landscape are the coastline and the mountains. In fact, it is the juxtaposition of sea and
mountains that makes it such a strikingly beautiful place. Mountains of up to 2,500 metres rise dramatically from the coast. My
apartment is only 20 minutes' walk from the sea and only just
above sea level. However, if I walk for less than 20 minutes inland, I am on the lower slopes of a 500 metre peak called Thilakas
(meaning 'enclave'), and in the distance I can see the Dhikti
Mountains, which rise to 2,000 metres and are snow-covered in

15

winter. We shall see later that this combination of sea and mountains has also had a major impact on the island's history.

Crete's location is geologically as well as historically significant. It is located at the point not only where three continents meet, but also, as Rackham and Moody point out, where 'two of the world's great continental plates are colliding'. 'Crete rides', they say, 'as if on the back of a bull, at the point where Africa burrows under Europe'.[3] In geological terms, Crete is relatively young. It was not formed until the end of the Permian era, approximately 50 million years ago, and is still in the process of evolution. This is reflected in a fairly high level of tectonic activity. During the Bronze Age, which was the time of the Minoan civilisation, there was apparently a particularly high degree of activity, including major earthquakes and a volcanic eruption in the neighbouring island of Santorini. Today there is less, but minor earthquakes are common. The island's relative youth also helps to explain its landscape, especially the dominance and form of the mountains.[4]

The whole of Crete's interior is mountainous. We shall see later that the mountains have had an important impact on people's lives and on the island's history. The more accessible lower slopes have always played an important role in rural livelihoods, including the cultivation of olives and grazing of livestock, and continue to do so today. The less accessible higher areas, with their rugged terrain and many caves, have been used as a refuge in times of invasion – most recently during the German invasion in the Second World War. And hill-tops and mountain peaks have always been revered and used as places of worship. Archaeological evidence suggests that in Minoan times many (including my 'local' hill Thilakas) were regarded as sacred, while today little chapels perched precariously on the top of hills are one of the most distinctive features of the Cretan landscape.

There are four main mountain blocks, or *massifs*: the White Mountains in the west (inland from Chania), the Psiloritis Mountains in the centre (between Rethymno and Iraklio), the Dhikti Mountains in Lasithi (between Iraklio and Aghios Nikolaos) and the Thryphti Mountains in the extreme east (between Aghios Niko- laos and Sitia). The White Mountains are generally regarded as the most impressive, with (according to Rackham and Moody) 'at least 20 peaks over 2,200 metres'.[5] However, the highest peak is Mount Ida, in the Psiloritis mountains, which rises to 2,456 me- tres. The two eastern *massifs* are slightly lower; the highest peak in the Dhikti Mountains is 2,148 metres and that in the Thriphti Mountains 'only' 1,476 metres. However, the eastern mountains are still very high - higher than Ben Nevis, for example, which is 1,344 metres. Moreover, in my view, they are more impressive than those further west because the island is narrower here and so the juxtaposition of coastline and mountains is particularly dramatic. Wherever you go on the coast, the mountains tower over you and if you go up into the mountains there are spectacu- lar views, including places where you can see both the north and south coasts.

Because its geological history is relatively recent, the moun- tain terrain is steep and rugged and there are many gorges and canyons. The best known gorge is the Samaria, which is on the southern slopes of the White Mountains. It is 13 kilometres long and a favourite spot for more energetic tourists, who usually walk down the gorge and then get a boat or bus on to their next destination. However, there are several impressive ones near Aghios Nikolaos. My favourite is the Cha Gorge, also known as the Cha Canyon.[6] It is a massive V-shaped cleft on the south- ern edge of the Thriphti Mountains, near the northern end of the road to Ierapetra. It is a major landmark, visible not only from places nearby but also from much further afield. I get a very good view of it from my 'local' beach on the outskirts of Aghios Nikolaos, and am constantly fascinated by the way in which its appearance changes, depending on the time of day and the light.

The geology of the mountains is complex, but the dominant rock is limestone. This is reflected in the existence of many caves and, in particular, in the drainage systems. There are very few perennial rivers on the island, partly because of the long dry season but also because many of the rivers flow underground. They disappear not far from their source, and only emerge when they reach the coast. My local beach provides a good example of this process. It is called *Almyros*, which means 'wetland', because it is at the point where an underground river system flows into the sea. According to Rackham and Moody, it is one of the three main wetlands on the island.[7] The river emerges from a spring just before it reaches the beach. A couple of hundred metres inland, there is no sign of it; but by the time it reaches the sea, it is a fast-flowing perennial river nearly ten metres wide. It emerges through a large expanse of reed-beds and, after heavy rain, other smaller streams also appear out of these beds and flow into the sea. Thanks to its mountainous terrain and, in particular, its underground drainage system, Crete has an abundant supply of water.

Another product of the island's geology is Lake Voulismeni, a deep natural lake in the centre of Aghios Nikolaos town. It is surrounded on three sides by steep cliffs and connected to the sea by a narrow channel. It is the focal point of the town. Restaurants line the shore and many cultural events are held there, including a spectacular pageant on Easter Saturday night which I will describe in a later chapter. There are many myths and stories about Lake Voulismeni. Some people say it is bottomless; others that in the 1950s a nearby earthquake caused a surge that sucked all the water out into the sea and then back in again several times. But according to a local British amateur geologist, it is about 60 metres deep. It was created by a former underground river (possibly part of the river system that now emerges at Almyros), that was displaced by a fault and thus created a deep 'sinkhole'. It used to be cut off from the sea and known as the 'stinky lake' because the water was stagnant; but in 1867 a channel was cut to link it to the sea and thus improve the water quality. The story about the earthquake is apparently partly true. There was a tidal wave, but it was only two metres high and the water was not sucked out of the lake.[8]

Crete's coastline is almost as dramatic as its mountains. Lovely beaches, often sandy but sometimes pebbly, alternate with rugged headlands, from which there are spectacular views. All the beaches are owned by the state and open to the general public. In 2014 the government, in an attempt to encourage investment, introduced a bill that would allow hotels or other businesses to claim stretches of coastline for their own exclusive use; but it was vehemently opposed and had to be withdrawn. The beaches are maintained by the local council and the more popular ones are equipped with outdoor showers, toilets and rentable sunbeds and sunshades.

The area around Aghios Nikolaos has some very good beaches. It is known as the Gulf of Mirabella and (as this name suggests) it is incredibly beautiful. Its beauty lies partly in the scenery, with its rocky cliffs, sandy beaches and mountain backdrop, but also in the sea itself, which is usually calm, very clear and deep aquamarine in colour. The town itself, which is built on a promontory, is a microcosm of the coastline as a whole: small sandy beaches separated by rocky headlands. Every road in the town leads to the beach – but to a different beach.

My local beach, Almyros, which is located outside the town on the road to Ierapetra and Sitia, is also my favourite one. There are several reasons why I like it: its long stretch of sand, the river and large expanse of reed-beds, the fact that it faces east and so gets the morning sun, and the panoramic view of the Thripthi Mountains, which form the south-eastern edge of the Gulf of Mirabella. And there is a very pleasant 15 minutes' walk along the coast from Almyros to the centre of town. Almyros is a designated conservation area because of the reed-beds, which are a habitat for many species of flora and fauna.

The only disadvantage of Almyros is that it is very crowded in summer. Although it is outside the town, there are several hotels nearby and it is also popular with local residents. One of the nice things about Crete's beaches is that they are used not just by tourists but also by the local people. In the summer they swim and sunbathe like everyone else and in winter they walk or run, exercise their dogs and fish on the beach. Like many popular beaches, Almyros is in many respects more attractive in winter, when there are very few people around and no sunbeds or sunshades. In summer, the best time to go is early in the morning or in the evening.

Crete's beaches are not all as heavily patronised as Almyros. One does not have to go far off the beaten track to find a quiet little cove where one might well be the only visitor. Moreover, they cater for a variety of tastes. In 2015, a beach known as Red Beach, located on the south coast near the town of Matala, came second in a competition to find the best nudist beach in the world![9] They also host a variety of activities, including pop concerts and discos. August is the favourite month for these events, which are patronised by both local people and tourists.

Almyros is a popular location for discos. On these occasions, a section of the beach is cordoned off and an entry fee charged – and of course, there is a bar. Like most forms of entertainment in Crete, these events start relatively late in the evening (usually around nine o'clock) and go on till the early hours of the morning. Although I have never actually attended one of these discos, I have on more than one occasion witnessed both the beginning and the end. When I went down to Almyros for an evening swim, the bar was being set up and the sound system tested and a few spectators were milling around. And when I returned the following day for my usual early morning dip, it appeared to have only just finished. Staff were dismantling the facilities and clearing up the heaps of rubbish, and a few drunken patrons were still propping up the bar, while others were fast asleep on the beach.

Although the mountains and coastline are the dominant land-scapes in Crete, they are not the only ones. There are also areas of relatively flat land, both on the coast and inland. The two main coastal plains are both on the south coast. One is the Mesara Plain, south of Iraklio, and the other the area around Ierapetra. They are interesting areas, partly because the topography is so different from the surrounding countryside but also because they produce large quantities of vegetables. Scenically, however, they are less attractive, because the vegetables are grown in plastic greenhouses (often known as 'polytunnels'). The number of greenhouses is particularly high in Ierapetra. When you come over the watershed from the north coast, you are greeted by a sea of plastic. There is a greenhouse on every available square metre of land, right down to the seashore. Economically, however, it is a very productive area.

The largest mountain plain is the Lasithi Plateau, which is in the Dhikti Mountains, about 25 kilometres west of Aghios Nikolaos. It is about 25 square kilometres in size and another important vegetable growing area. The name 'plateau' is misleading because it is actually surrounded by mountains. It is about 800 metres in altitude, while the mountains around it reach over 2,000 metres. There are only two roads up to it, one from the north and one from the east, and both are long, winding and in places precipitous. However, although it is not an easy drive, it is well worth the effort. There are spectacular views as you go up the mountains and then, when you reach the top of the pass, you look down on a vast expanse of flat agricultural land. The plateau itself is also interesting. It is known not only for its vegetables but also as a centre of traditional culture. The landscape is dotted with windmills, although they are no longer in use, and on the south-eastern edge, near the village of Psychro, there is a massive limestone cave, which was a centre of worship from Minoan times. And when one finally reaches the plateau, travel is easy. There is a good circular road around the edge, linking the many small villages, and a network of minor farm roads.

Climate

> So much for a typical season; but few seasons are
> typical. (Rackham and Moody, 1996, p.33)

Crete has a Mediterranean climate. I was taught at school that the main characteristics of such a climate are 'hot, dry, dusty summers and warm wet winters with the west wind blowing'. That provides a general indication of what to expect; but, as the above quotation suggests, the island's climate is actually far more complex. There are enormous variations, not only from one year to the next but also from one part of the island to another. These variations are due to its location, its size and shape, and its topography.

The island's location is of strategic importance. As Rackham and Moody point out, 'Crete lies at the junction of four great weather systems'. In summer, they explain, 'it comes between the Azores High and the Indo-Persian Low', which combine to create dry, sunny weather and north-westerly winds. In winter, it is caught between low pressure in the Atlantic and high pressure over south-west Asia and North Africa. This creates periods of very wet, windy weather, interspersed with dry, sunny spells.[10] Furthermore, these basic patterns are tempered both by the sea, which is never far away in Crete, and the mountainous topography. The sea moderates temperatures and affects the direction of the wind, which tends to blow off the sea during the day and off the land at night, while the topography leads to enormous variations in both temperature and rainfall, the former due to altitude and the latter due to the effect of rain shadow.

The table below provides some temperature and rainfall data for seven locations: three on the north coast (Chania in the west, Iraklio in the centre and Sitia in the east), two on or near the south coast (Gortyn in the centre and Ierapetra in the east), and two in the mountains (Anogeia in the centre and Tzermiadhon further east, on the Lasithi Plateau). As the table shows, temperatures are noticeably higher on the south coast than on the north and much higher on the coast than in the mountains. Similarly, rainfall is significantly higher in the west than the east and increases dramatically with altitude.

Crete: Temperature and Rainfall Data

Location	Mean temp. in hottest month (°C)	Mean temp.in coldest month (°C)	Highest recorded temp. (°C)	Lowest recorded temp. (°C)	Mean annual rainfall (mm)
Chania	26.9	11.9	42.0	-1.0	657
Iraklio	26.4	12.3	45.7	-0.5	492
Sitia	26.4	12.7	42.2	0	505
Gortyn	28.3	11.0	44.2	-0.8	564
Ierapetra	28.1	12.9	44.0	1.0	432
Anogeia	23.3	7.3	41.2	-5.8	1134
Tzermiadhon	20.4	5.7	38.2	-15.4	1236

Source: Rackham, O. and J. Moody, 1996, p.34.

In all areas, most of the rain falls in winter, particularly between December and February. In the mountains it often falls as snow and the higher peaks are snow-capped throughout the winter. At sea-level snow is rare, occurring on average only once in ten years according to Rackham and Moody.[11] However, hail is common.

I do not have any climate data for Aghios Nikolaos. However, I have kept records of the maximum and minimum daily temperatures at my home for two years and recorded the rainfall for about 18 months. Although these are obviously of no long-term statistical value, they give some idea of what the weather is like on a day-to-day basis. In July and August, which are the hottest months, the maximum day-time temperature ranged from 26° to

36° while at night the minimum ranged from 21° to 30°. And in the three coldest months, December, January and February, the maximum ranged from 6° to 22° and the minimum from 1.5° to 17°. Somewhat surprisingly, the lowest temperature (1.5°) was on 19 February 2015, at the time when one is expecting the weather to begin to get warmer.

The total rainfall for the 2014 calendar year was 485 mms, which is midway between the official figures for Iraklio and Ierapetra and thus probably fairly typical. However, the use of the calendar year is in this case misleading because it includes parts of two very different rainy seasons (2013-14 and 2014-15). In 2013-14, the rainfall for the three wettest months (December to February) was 195 mms, while in 2014-15 it was 684 mms. The winter of 2014-15 was unusually cold and wet and it actually snowed twice in Aghios Nikolaos. The first snowfall was in early January and the second during the cold spell in the middle of February. People said that it was the first snow for ten years, which supports Rackham and Moody's data. In terms of the distribution of rainfall, it is also interesting to note that, although most of the rain in 2014 was, as one would expect, in the winter, there was some precipitation every month except July.

My recordings also demonstrate the enormous variations in the weather, not just from one year to another but also from one day to the next. It is not uncommon, especially in the autumn and winter, for temperatures to drop ten degrees or more in a matter of hours. This happens when one air mass meets another. The drop in temperature is usually preceded by heavy rain, together with thunder, lightning and high winds. On both occasions when it snowed in Aghios Nikolaos, the snow was accompanied by thunder storms. Moreover, between the two cold spells there was a period of relatively mild weather, including a day in which the temperature went up to 20°.

The wind is another significant characteristic of the climate. Because of its island location, Crete is nearly always windy. The question is not whether it is windy, but how strong the wind is and, in particular, which way it is blowing. Although the predominant wind direction is north or north-west, it can actually blow from any direction and the most significant difference is between a northerly wind and a southerly one. The impact of this difference depends on the season. In summer, a cool north wind can be very pleasant, since it makes the heat less oppressive, while a south wind is warm and moist and thus makes it feel even hotter. In winter, however, a north wind is bitterly cold, while a south wind brings wet but relatively mild weather. The impact of wind speed also depends on the season. In summer, when the earth is dry, a strong wind is unpleasant because it creates dust storms, while in winter, a strong wind may be unpleasantly cold but at least it dries things out a little.

The impact of the wind is such that at any particular point in time there are significant differences between the weather on the north coast and that on the south coast. One of the advantages of living, as I do, near the narrowest point in the island, is that one can move from one side to the other, depending on the weather. For example, if one wants to go to the beach and in Aghios Nikolaos there is a cold wind blowing and the sea is rough, one can drive across to the south coast, where the beach will probably be sheltered and the sea calm.

As this example suggests, the vagaries of Crete's climate have a significant effect on its inhabitants. In the next section we will see how they have affected the flora and fauna and in later chapters we will explore other aspects of their impact on human activity, from Minoan times to the present era.

Flora and Fauna

[Crete's] present appearance is the result of millennia of interaction between human activities, human default, and the workings of Nature. (Rackham, O. and J. Moody,

25

The Making of the Cretan Landscape, Manchester University Press, 1996, p.xi)

In Crete it is difficult to talk about the 'natural' flora or fauna. There has been human settlement and cultivation for more than 7,000 years and, as the above quotation suggests, there is evidence of man's activity everywhere. Consequently, it is often difficult to distinguish the 'natural' from the 'cultivated' or 'domesticated' and the 'indigenous' from the 'introduced'. This applies both to individual plants and animals and to overall patterns of land use.

Soon after I moved to Crete, I spent a month in New Zealand. The contrast with Crete could not be greater. New Zealand is much more remote than Crete and so has a unique flora and fauna. Moreover, it is unusual in that there was no human settlement there until the 13th century, so the importation of non-indigenous species of plants and animals is a relatively recent phenomenon. However, many of these imported species have thrived in the New Zealand environment and thus pose a major threat to the indigenous flora and fauna and this has led to a massive conservation programme.

I appreciated the objectives of the programme and was impressed by the commitment to it, not just by the government but also by the general public. However, I was taken aback by the nature and extent of the measures used. Any non-indigenous species of plant that grows wild or semi-wild is referred to not as a 'wild flower' but as a 'weed' and similarly any non-indigenous species of wild animal is regarded not as 'wildlife' but as a 'feral' animal. And these weeds and feral animals are ruthlessly eradicated. This includes the annual slaughter of thousands of rabbits, deer and feral goats. I could not help wondering whether the ends of the programme justify the means. In Crete, as in many other parts of the 'old world', the flora and fauna are a complex mixture of indigenous and non-indigenous species, and is this such a bad thing?

Flora

According to *The Atlas of Crete*, which is another valuable source of information on the physical environment, there are approximately 1,700 species of plants in Crete.[12] However, to a layman (or laywoman) like myself, there are two dominant types of vegetation. These are olive groves and *maquis*.

Olive groves are probably the most distinctive feature of the Cretan landscape. They are found on every available piece of land up to about 750 metres, including suburban gardens. They are the dominant tree crop. As the *Atlas* points out, 'the percentage of wooded landscape in Crete is quite high if you include the taller shrubs and extensive olive groves – or, alternatively, startlingly low if you leave them out'.[13]

The olive is a prime example of the difficulty in distinguishing both between 'natural' and 'cultivated' and between 'indigenous' and 'introduced' species. Olives are undoubtedly a cultivated crop and, in fact, they are the island's most important crop. However, since they are grown everywhere, often with little or no maintenance, one is tempted to regard them as 'natural' vegetation. Their origin is unknown. Some sources suggest that they originated in North Africa and were imported to Crete via Egypt, but Rackham and Moody say there is evidence that they are indigenous.[14] Whatever the case, they have been here so long that they are an integral part of the vegetation. Crete is believed to be one of the first places (the others being Syria and Palestine) where olives were cultivated. There is evidence of their cultivation in the late Neolithic period, which is 4,400-3,500 BC. The trees themselves are also often very old. According to Rackham and Moody, they are 'perhaps the longest-lived crop plant'; their book has a photograph of a tree in western Crete that is believed to be more than 2,000 years old.[15]

Maquis is a vague term, used to refer to a variety of different types of scrubland in the Mediterranean. It is found in areas where the quality of the soil and/or the rainfall is insufficient to support larger plants, and in those where the primary vegetation has been destroyed, for example by grazing or fire. In Crete it is found in two main locations: along the coast and on the hills and lower slopes of the mountains.

This scrubland actually includes three types of plants: stunted trees, shrubs and herbaceous plants. Rackham and Moody use the term *maquis* to refer only to the first of these;[16] but since all three tend to be found in the same place, it is often used to refer to the overall vegetation system. Within each category of plant, there are many different species, depending on region and local conditions. The combination of the three types results in a dense ground cover that is difficult to penetrate, particularly since some of the plants have thorns or sharp twigs that scratch the skin.

Although olive groves and *maquis* dominate the Cretan landscape, they are not the only form of vegetation. There are many areas of 'proper' woodland, particularly in the western part of the island where the rainfall is higher, but also in the east. Indigenous tree species include Cretan pine, cypress, various oaks (both evergreen and deciduous), two types of junipers (which Rackham and Moody refer to as 'land-juniper' and 'sea-juniper') and Cretan palm.[17]

There are several interesting areas of native woodland within easy reach of Aghios Nikolaos. One is Kroustas Forest, a pine forest on the lower slopes of the mountains south-west of the town, near the village of Kroustas. Another is Chrisi Island, a small island off the coast of Ieraptera, which is home to one of the largest natural collections of sea-junipers in the Mediterranean. There is, however, some confusion over the identity of these trees, with many guidebooks referring to them as cedars. This confusion appears to stem from the fact that in Greek the word for 'juniper' and 'cedar' is the same. They are both called κέδρος! This seems odd, since the two trees are very different, but so far I have failed to find an explanation. A little further away, at the extreme eastern end of the island, fringing one of the island's most acclaimed sandy beaches, there is the Vai palm forest. It covers an area of about 25 hectares and is said to be the largest palm forest in Europe. There is also some confusion about this forest. It is often claimed that it was introduced by the Arabs who occupied the island between 823 and 961 AD, but Rackham and Moody (and others) are confident that it is indigenous. Both Chrisi Island and Vai are popular tourist destinations.

Other significant types of natural vegetation include the reed-beds, which I have already mentioned, the wild flowers and the herbs. The island is renowned for the spectacular carpets of wild flowers that appear as if from nowhere in spring. They include daisies, anemones, irises, buttercups and many others, and come in a variety of colours – white, yellow, blue, red, purple. And they occur everywhere: on the cliff tops, on hill and mountain slopes, and on cultivated land. Although the majority are indigenous, the most prolific is an introduced species, a brilliant yellow flower known both as Bermuda buttercup and Cape sorrell. As these alternative names suggest, this is another case where there is some confusion over the plant's origins. But the general opinion seems to be that it comes from South Africa. According to Rackham and Moody, it 'so completely carpets the olive-groves in spring that it is prominent in pictures from space'.[18] However, it does not seem to have done much damage to the indigenous vegetation and provides a useful source of animal fodder. Moreover, like the other wild flowers, it disappears as quickly as it comes. But I dread to think what its fate would be in New Zealand!

Crete is also renowned for its herbs, which are sometimes cultivated but also grow wild. They are used for both culinary and medicinal purposes and play an important role in Cretan culture. Common species include thyme, sage, oregano, savory, camomile and lavender. There is a particular type of oregano, known as *diktamo* or dittany, which is found only in Crete. It is used for medicinal purposes, usually in the form of tea, but is also said to be an aphrodisiac.

There are, of course, also many cultivated plants, most of which have been introduced from elsewhere but usually long ago. Some are grown for their produce and others for decoration. It is neither possible nor necessary to describe all of them here. However, I will mention a few in order to give some idea both of the range of plants and of their contribution to the island's attractions; and I will also discuss some of them further in later chapters.

The most important tree crops other than olives are the various types of citrus. Oranges are so prolific that in December and January, which is the main harvest season, they are left rotting on trees and in the streets. Other tree crops include common temperate fruit like apples, pears and plums, but also more exotic species, such as loquats, chestnuts, mulberries, carob and, in some areas, avocados and bananas. Non-tree crops include a wide variety of vegetables, fruits such as strawberries, melons and water melons – and, of course, grapes. Grapes have been grown since Minoan times and are an essential part of Cretan culture. They are grown primarily for wine, but also for the fruit. They grow so prolifically that in the main harvest season, which is around July, one can pick fruit from vines growing semi-wild or abandoned along the sides of roads. Grains, including wheat, were an important crop in the past. However, since neither the climate nor the terrain is very suitable for grain crops and imported produce is readily available, cultivation is now limited to small quantities of barley.

A wide variety of trees and shrubs are grown primarily for decorative purposes and there are some flowers in bloom at almost all times of the year. Two of the most common are oleander and bougainvillea. Oleander is widely used as a hedge plant and along the sides of roads, partly because it is drought resistant, but also because it is poisonous and apparently goats know this and so don't eat it. Bougainvillea is usually found growing up the sides of buildings. One of the archetypical Cretan scenes, frequently reproduced on postcards, is a white-walled house, with blue doors and shutters, bedecked with a mass of pink or red bougainvillea. In the postcards, there is often also a wizened old man or woman sitting outside the door.

Two other notable trees are mimosas and tamarix. Mimosas are often planted along the sides of roads. They produce a mass of brilliant yellow flowers in the spring. Tamarix grow along the seashore. Although an introduced species, they grow more or less wild. They provide an attractive backdrop to many beaches – and a valuable source of shade on a hot day. And finally, brief mention should be made of the many sweet smelling flowers. These include orange and lemon blossom, jasmine and frangipani. Frangipani, which is abundant in Africa, is one of my favourite flowers. In Crete it is found mainly on the warmer south coast but I have successfully cultivated some in my garden.

Fauna

As I mentioned earlier, there are some similarities between the island of Crete and Africa's Lake Kariba, not just in their size and shape but also in the beauty of the scenery. When it comes to wildlife, however, the two are very different. One of Kariba's main attractions is the abundance of wildlife, including large mammals such as elephants, lions and hippopotamus, a great variety of birds, and several species of reptile – and their presence is evident wherever one goes. In Crete, however, the wildlife population is much more limited, both in quantity and in variety, and its presence less obvious. Apparently, however, this has not always been the case. According to Rackham and Moody, during the Pleistocene period there was a much wider range of wildlife, including 'an elephant the size of a bullock' and 'a pig-sized hippopotamus'![19]

The largest wild land mammal in Crete today, and the only one unique to the island, is the Cretan wild goat, or *agrimi*, commonly translated into English as *kri-kri*. Although once common in all mountainous areas, extensive hunting has reduced numbers almost to the point of extinction. It is now confined to the mountains of western Crete and some small islands to which some animals were moved in the 1920s as a conservation measure. Rackham and Moody say that it is probably not indigenous but was introduced during the Minoan era.[20]

There are a variety of smaller land mammals, including rats, mice, rabbits, hares, weasels, martens, hedgehogs, wild cats and badgers. Some of these are sub-species unique to Crete. There are also several species of bat and, in the sea, there are whales, dolphins and seals. Unfortunately, however, in much of the island, one is more likely to see these animals dead than alive. As is so often the case with wildlife in populated areas, they are most often seen as 'road kill' - in other words, run over by vehicles.

Unfortunately, there are no comprehensive books on the birds of Crete. The best attempt is a handy little book by George Sfikas, called *Birds and Mammals of Crete*, which (as its name suggests) is also a useful guide to the mammal population.[21] There are, however, a number of websites that list the various species of bird found on the island. According to one of these, *Avibase*,[22] 356 different species have been recorded. This relatively large number reflects the fact that Crete is a stopping place for many birds that migrate between Europe and Africa. For me, this is the most interesting aspect of bird life, partly because of the great variety of birds that one sees and the variation from one time of year to another, but also because it is a good example of Crete's strategic location.

There are no birds unique to Crete. Most of the species seen on the island can also be found in other parts of Europe. They include many familiar English 'garden' birds, such as blackbirds, thrushes, sparrows, chaffinches, wrens, and (although less common) robins. However, most of these species are, at least in populated areas, less abundant than in England. The only birds I see frequently in my garden are sparrows, blackbirds and a shy little bird, more common here than in the UK, called a blackcap. According to Sfikas, some of these species practise a form of seasonal migration within Crete, spending the winters in the lowlands and the summers in the mountains. This certainly appears to be the case with blackbirds, which I see or hear frequently between October and May, but never in the height of summer. Other common birds include wood pigeons and doves, swallows in summer, and the ubiquitous hooded crow.

The coasts and inland waters are home to a variety of water birds, such as gulls, egrets, cormorants, kingfishers and geese, while the mountains are renowned for their birds of prey, including relatively rare species of eagles and vultures. And, although most of the birds in Crete are found elsewhere in Europe, in summer one may apparently see some species that are native to Africa, including hoopoes, bee-eaters and rollers. However, I have yet to see any of these myself.

In general, I have been somewhat disappointed by the bird life in Crete. Both inland and on the coast, there appear to be fewer birds than one would see in similar environments in the UK. One reason for this is said to be their popularity as a source of food. In the past, birds were frequently hunted for food and, although the hunting of 'song birds' is now prohibited, some no doubt continues. And in built-up areas there are large numbers of cats, which are no doubt partly to blame. In some cases, however, I suspect that the birds are there but just not easily visible. This is certainly the case in the reed-beds at Almyros, which are so tall and dense that one never catches more than a glimpse of any of the birds or other wildlife that live there.

Of the many other forms of wildlife, three warrant brief mention. First are the loggerhead turtles, which live in the sea but emerge onto the beaches at night to lay their eggs. They are relatively rare and a protected species. They are found mainly on the north coast, between Iraklio and Rethymno, and there are signs on the beaches there warning tourists not to disturb their nests. Second are the snails, which spend the long dry summers asleep on a sheltered tree or wall and then suddenly come to life when it starts to rain. They are a popular food among many Cretans. The third is the *cicada*, which is a kind of beetle. It is notable because of the noise it makes, which is similar to that of a cricket, but made not by rubbing the legs together (as with crickets) but by contracting the muscles of the abdomen. Cicadas live in trees (including olive trees), and although they are seldom seen, their constant chirping is one of the most distinctive sounds in Crete, as in other parts of the Mediterranean. Moreover, since they only appear when it is hot, the first sound of *cicadas* (usually in late May or early June) is a sign that summer has come.

On the positive side, there are no forms of wildlife that pose a serious threat to humans. There are apparently four species of snake but they are seldom seen and, although one is venomous, it is not life-threatening.[23] There is the usual assortment of insects, including some, such as mosquitoes, scorpions and cockroaches, which can be unpleasant. However, the mosquitoes do not carry malaria, so they are merely a nuisance, not a health hazard; the scorpions are few and far between; and (as elsewhere) cockroaches tend to be found only in places that are not kept clean.

In addition to the wildlife, there are significant numbers of domesticated animals in Crete. Most important are the sheep and goats. Rackham and Moody estimate that at the time they wrote their book (1996), there were about 700,000 sheep and 300,000 goats – that is, equivalent to more than one sheep and about half a goat per head of the population. The domesticated goats are smaller than the wild ones and, unlike the poor 'feral' goats in New Zealand, play an important part in the local economy and are highly valued. Traditional grazing patterns include the movement of sheep and goats (like the blackbirds) between lower and higher altitudes depending on the season, a practice known as *transhumance*. There are very few cattle, but some people keep pigs and donkeys are still used as a means of transport in rural areas. Many people also rear poultry, including not only chickens but also turkeys and guinea fowl, and some keep ducks or geese, while other forms of animal husbandry include the keeping of rabbits and bees. I will discuss the nature and role of these activities further in later chapters.

In conclusion, I should perhaps say something about Crete's cat population. The Cretan wild cat is, like the Cretan wild goat, now extremely rare; but, as I have already indicated, there is an abundance of domesticated cats. Some of these are household pets, fed and cared for by a particular family. But many are not. They live in built-up areas but lead a semi-wild existence, surviving on household scraps (sometimes given to them, but more often scrounged from dustbins) and any birds or small mammals they can catch. They are often in poor condition, but because they are not neutered, they breed prolifically. I will say more about the 'problem' of these 'feral' cats in Chapter 6.

Conclusion

For the purposes of this book, the most important point that has hopefully emerged from this brief review of the geography of Crete is that it is a land of contrasts and extremes. More specifically, it is a land that both attracts and repels. We shall see in subsequent chapters that, throughout its history, 'outsiders' have been attracted to the island, partly by its strategic location but also by its resources, including its harbours and beaches, beautiful scenery and productive agricultural land. Consequently, Crete has been subject to repeated invasions, which have had a dramatic effect on its economy and culture. Moreover, it has often been a battleground – not only for the struggles between colliding tectonic plates and clashing weather systems described in this chapter, but also for those between conflicting geopolitical interests. However, there are also aspects of Crete's physical environment, such as the mountainous terrain and climatic extremes, which repel outsiders. We shall see that these factors, together with the resilience of the Cretan people, have limited the

extent to which invaders have been able to penetrate the island and enabled the local population to maintain a remarkably high degree of identity and autonomy.

Chapter 3

History: A Tale of Invasion and Resistance

Fortunate is he who studied history. (Euripides)

I am not a historian. When I was at school, I did not like history. I think there were two reasons for this. One was the way it was taught. In my O-level history lessons, the teacher merely dictated long lists of dates and events, which we had to copy and learn by heart. This must have been a good way of getting us to pass the exam, since (much to my surprise) my highest mark was for history. But it didn't stimulate either an interest in the subject or an appreciation of its importance. The other reason, however, was that history doesn't mean so much when one is young. It is only as I have grown older that I have come to appreciate its value.

I now realise that a knowledge of history is essential in order to understand the present. I learned this the hard way, through forty years of practical experience in international development. When I began my career, many African and Asian countries had just become politically independent. For the governments and peoples of those countries, and for the many expatriates like myself who rushed in to help them, independence was seen as a new start. We failed to realise that the future progress of these countries was, at least in part, limited by their past. This is what academics call 'path dependency'.

In Crete, one cannot ignore history. There are two reasons for this. The first is that wherever one goes there are reminders of the island's past. Although in terms of geology Crete is a relatively new part of the world, when it comes to history it is one of the oldest. It is renowned for being the home of the Minoan empire, which is generally regarded as the oldest civilisation in Europe, and there are Minoan archaeological sites all over the island, together with relics from more recent eras. The second reason why history is so important is that its impact is evident in so many aspects of life today. It was the realisation of this that led me to write this book.

Crete's history is complex, not only because it goes back a very long way, but also because it is characterised by successive waves of occupation. Over the centuries, it has been occupied by many different external powers, including Greeks, Romans, Byzantines, Arabs, Venetians, Turks, Egyptians, Germans, Italians and (if one includes the time when it was an international protectorate) Britain, France and Russia. Each of these occupations constitutes a different chapter in the story. I have divided the island's history into the following phases, each of which corresponds to a section of the chapter:

1. Pre-Minoan (12000-2700 BC) and Minoan (2700-1100 BC) eras;
2. Colonisation by mainland Greeks (1450-67 BC);
3. Roman occupation (69 BC – 395 AD);
4. Byzantine (325-827; 961-1204) and Arab (827--961) occupations;
5. Venetian occupation (1204-1671);

6. Turkish (Ottoman) occupation (1669-1897);
7. Cretan autonomy under international protection (1897-1913);
8. Incorporation into modern Greece (1913-present).

The dates given above are generally accepted and widely used. However, they should be treated with caution because, as we shall see in due course, there was seldom a clear division between one phase and the next; in most cases, it was a gradual transition. In some cases, this is indicated by an overlap in dates.

One of the main problems with history is that it is not an objective science. There are three interrelated problems. Firstly, although there are some generally agreed 'facts', most of the material on which historical studies are based is subjective in nature. It is derived from observations and records that vary in quality and inevitably only present part of the story. Secondly, it is not always possible to separate 'history' and 'myth'. This is particularly but not only so in the case of ancient history. Thirdly, all historical studies have an element of bias, because the historian has to decide what material to include (even which 'facts') and how to interpret it. This in turn means that history is inevitably used (and abused) to achieve particular objectives; for example, to support an argument, portray an historical period in a particular light, or promote a sense of ethnic or national identity.

In my case, I have tried to present a relatively balanced view. However, I have had to be selective and have obviously focused on those aspects of Crete's history that relate to my central argument. Moreover, I have been limited by the quantity and quality of the available sources. There is surprisingly little material on the history of Crete written in English, and in particular very little recent material. And the sources that are available are fraught with the problems described above. For example, there is much more material about some periods than others, there are places where history and myth are intertwined, and some of the sources present a very obviously biased picture. However, these problems are in themselves interesting and of relevance to my argument. My main source has been Theocharis Detorakis' *History of* Crete, which was published in 1994 and is the only comprehensive book available.[24] I have also made extensive use of Michael Llewellyn Smith's *Crete: The Great Island*, which provides some interesting insights but was published fifty years ago, focuses on cultural aspects and is, as he says, a personal view,[25] and Manolis Makrakis' *Elounda, Spinalonga, Agios Nikolaos: Their History*, which is a more recent publication and provides a good account of the history of my local area.[26] I have also drawn on a variety of other sources, including guide books, information in museums and on the internet, and historical novels.

Since this book is not intended to be a historical text, I have tried to summarise Crete's long and complex history as briefly and simply as possible, and in so doing have had to omit many details and oversimplify many issues. Nevertheless, this is still a long chapter and some readers may find it daunting. I would encourage such readers to persist, because some knowledge of Crete's history is essential not just to follow my argument but also to appreciate the Crete of today. However, anyone who finds it too onerous may jump to the final section, in which I summarise the main points and discuss the implications for Part Two of the book.

Indigenous Crete

> 'She is thirty-five,' added the Mother Superior with a
> sigh. 'An unhappy age – very difficult! May the Holy
> Martyred Virgin come to her aid and cure her! In ten or
> fifteen years she will be cured.'
> 'Ten or fifteen years,' I murmured, aghast.
> 'What are ten or fifteen years?' asked the Mother
> Superior severely. 'Think of eternity!'
> (Nikos Kazantzakis, *Zorba the Greek,* Faber and Faber,
> *1961, p. 188*)

Another advantage of studying history is that, like the above quotation from *Zorba the Greek*, it makes one think about the concept of time. This is particularly so in Crete, which has such a long history. It is undoubtedly one of the cradles of civilisation. In 2009 an archaeological exploration in Plakias, on the south coast, found relics of a stone-age culture dating back to at least 12,000 BC.[27] There is evidence of agriculture as far back as 5,000 BC, which is only two thousand years later than areas like Egypt and Iraq, and the Minoan civilisation, for which Crete is renowned, is thought to have emerged between 3,000 and 2,000 BC. It is difficult to believe, when walking around one of the many relatively well preserved Minoan sites, that these settlements were built thousands of years ago. It is so far back in time that it makes one think of eternity.

Minoan society is, as I have already mentioned, widely regarded as the first 'civilisation' in Europe. 'Civilisation' is a vague term that is used in many different ways. However, in this context, it generally refers to a society where the development of agriculture has led to a division of labour, and thus to the emergence of urban settlements, arts and crafts, a class structure, and some form of government. The Minoan society certainly classifies as a civilisation in terms of these criteria. There is evidence of clearly demarcated urban settlements that thrived on the basis of agricultural produce from nearby rural areas, of 'palaces' that are presumed to have been the homes of a ruling elite, arts and crafts such as pottery, and the development of a written language.

The most famous Minoan site is the palace of Knossos, which is located a few kilometres inland from the present town of Iraklio. Knossos was excavated and partially restored at the beginning of the 20th century by Arthur Evans, a British archaeologist. It is interesting for tourists because some sections of it have been reconstructed in an attempt to give some idea of how the palace would originally have looked and what life would have been like there. However, many of the assumptions Evans made about Minoan culture are now being challenged. This is reflected in the information signs explaining what the various buildings and artefacts are, many of which point out this was only what Evans assumed they were.

Arthur Evans has played a major role in determining our knowledge of the Minoan civilisation and the fact that his views are now being challenged is a good example of the subjectivity involved in the writing of history. It was Evans who actually gave the civilisation its name. He believed that Knossos was the palace of the mythical king, Minas, and thus named the civilisation 'Minoan'. However, no one actually knows whether King Minas ever existed and, if he did, where his 'palace' was. Like King Arthur, there are many myths about King Minas but no conclusive evidence of his existence.

Arthur Evans' role reminds me of the way in which anthropologists influenced our knowledge of 'less developed' societies during the 20th Century. In the 1970s I spent six years in Papua New Guinea. Since a large part of its population had only recently come into contact with modern 'civilisation', the country was an anthropologist's paradise. However, while I was there, views about anthropologists began to change. As Papua New Guineans from these 'primitive' communities became educated and thus able to tell their own stories, it emerged that the anthropologists had often misunderstood or misinterpreted many aspects of the societies in which they lived and worked. It is therefore hardly surprising that archaeologists like Arthur Evans should suffer a similar fate.

Knossos is only one of innumerable Minoan sites on the island. One of the amazing aspects of Minoan culture is that there are many more relics of it than of any of the later phases of Cretan history. One cannot travel far without coming across a site. Although many are preserved as historical sites, others are not even marked on a map. Some are not easy to recognise. For example, in a coastal area called Istron, a few kilometres south of Aghios Nikolaos, where I often go for walks, there is what looks like the foundations of some old building. It was not until I went there with a local resident that I learned that it was a Minoan site.

A few kilometres beyond Istron, on the road leading to Ierapetra and Sitia, is the site of a large Minoan town called Gournia. It is one of the best-preserved Minoan sites and the layout of the buildings is still clearly visible. In my view, it is more impressive than Knossos because there has been no attempt to reconstruct any of the buildings. One is therefore able to imagine for oneself what it might have been like – and to appreciate how remarkable it is that such relics still exist today. Moreover, there are incredible views from the site, both back along the coast towards Aghios Nikolaos and inland to the hills that form the watershed between the north and south coasts.

Most of the Minoan archaeological explorations have been of urban sites; that is, of towns like Gournia and palaces like Knossos. However, in the Kroustas Forest, which I mentioned in Chapter 2, a German archaeologist, Sabine Beckmann, has recently studied the rural society.[28] Her work is apparently one of the first archaeological studies of rural settlements. From the remains of stone buildings, pottery and other artefacts, she has deduced quite a lot of information about the inhabitants of the area, who lived in scattered homesteads, grew barley, and kept sheep, goats and bees. It was from her that I learned that Thilakas, the hill that I see from my house, was a sacred place.

There has been some dispute over the origins of the Minoans. Until recently, archaeologists assumed that they were migrants from regions where similar civilisations already existed. Arthur Evans, noting similarities between Egyptian and Minoan pottery, suggested that they came from the Nile Delta, while others claimed that they were from Syria, Palestine or Turkey. However, it is now believed that the civilisation was indigenous, emerging independently from the earlier Neolithic cultures. This conclusion is based on an analysis of DNA samples from skeletons from the Minoan era found in a cave in the Lasithi Plateau, which show a resemblance not with Egyptian or Middle Eastern peoples but with those of neighbouring parts of southern Europe.[29] That is why I have called this section 'indigenous Crete'.

However, there is no doubt that contact with areas like Egypt and the Middle East contributed to both the evolution and the prosperity of Minoan civilisation. There is archaeological evidence of trade within the eastern Mediterranean as far back as 3,000 BC and the Minoans were undoubtedly a trading nation. This is now believed to explain the similarities between Egyptian and Minoan pottery that led Arthur Evans to suggest that the Minoans came from Egypt. Thus, even at this early stage of its history, Crete's strategic position at the eastern end of the Mediterranean had an important impact on its development. There is also, of course, the question of where the original inhabitants of Cretans originated, but that was a very long time ago.

The island's topography also played an important role at this time. Most of the Minoan towns were located in strategic positions, often on hills overlooking the coast. Gournia is a particularly good example. It is located on the north coast, but near the narrowest point in the island, so with easy access also to the south coast and in a position where it could defend itself from invaders from any direction. The DNA studies from the Lasithi Plateau also provide interesting insights into the importance of the mountains. The DNA samples from the Minoan skeletons were found to be almost identical to those of the Plateau's present inhabitants, suggesting that the area has long been a refuge to which the indigenous population has fled to escape from invaders. .

Archaeologists divide the Minoan era into five phases: the 'prepalatian' (2700-1900 BC), the 'old palatial' (1900-1700 BC), the 'new palatial' (1700-1450 BC), the 'final palatial' (1450-1300 BC), and the 'post palatial' (1300-1150 BC). The pre-palatian period was one in which there was little stratification of society and no centralised authority. The old palatial was the time when a centralised system of government began to emerge and the first palaces were built. This society collapsed suddenly for reasons that are not clear. It was once thought that it was destroyed by the eruption of the volcano Thera on the neighbouring island of Santorini, but the timing of this does not seem to fit. Other possible causes include earthquakes, fire, outside invasion and internal conflicts. Whatever the causes, the society was rebuilt and the new palatial period was the height of the Minoan civilisation. This was the time that Knossos was built and, so we are told, exerted its authority over the whole island. During the final palatial period, the centralised structure of society began gradually to break down, again for reasons that are not clear, and in the post-palatial period Crete resorted to a nation of small, semi-autonomous rural settlements.

The last two phases are characterised also by the increasing presence of Mycenaean Greeks from the mainland, who took over the control of Knossos in 1450 BC. Among other things, they brought with them a new form of script, which is known as Linear B to distinguish it from the Minoan script, known as Linear A. This period thus marks both the end of the Minoan era and the beginning of the next chapter in the island's history – that of Greek colonisation. Hence the overlap in dates between the two periods.

The Greek Colonisation

> Greek colonisation is a multi-faceted phenomenon without a strictly defined beginning or end. It developed over several centuries in the form of waves of migrations of Greeks to west and east. (Exhibition at Archaeological Museum of Thessaloniki, December 2014)

> There is a land called Crete in the midst of the winedark sea, a fair land and a rich, begirt with water, and therein are many men innumerable and ninety cities. (Homer, *The Odyssey*, Book XIX)

This period in the island's history has received much less attention than the Minoan era. This is understandable for two reasons.
Firstly, there is less visible archaeological evidence. Secondly,
and probably more importantly, Crete was no longer the centre
of a civilisation, as it was in the Minoan era, but on the margins
of another civilisation – that of ancient Greece. Consequently,
most literature about the period, including that by scholars of
the time and by historians, focuses on the centre of the empire,
which was the Greek mainland. We shall see later in the chapter
that this was to be the case for much of the rest of the island's history. As Rackham and Moody say, 'Crete was always an outlying
province'.[30]

However, the lack of attention given to this era is in my view
unfortunate because it was one of the most important periods in
the history of western civilisation, a time when there were major
advances in science, philosophy, art, literature and governance.
Moreover, the archaeological and documentary information
available suggests that it was also a critical time in Crete's history and that, despite its marginal position, the island played an
important role in the evolution of the Greek Empire.

The spread of the ancient Greek civilisation was, as the first of the
above quotations suggests, characterised by waves of migration
and occupation. The quotation is from an exhibition on Greek
colonisation and, although it refers specifically to the last phase
of the Greek empire (known as the Hellenic period), its relevance
is much wider. In fact, the purpose of the exhibition was to demonstrate that, throughout history, Greeks have migrated to other
parts of the world, taking their culture with them and thereby
contributing to the development of other societies. This was, I
think, intended to throw a positive light on the latest wave of
migrations, which (as we shall see later) was driven by the country's economic collapse in 2009.

Historians generally divide the history of ancient Greece into
five main phases: the Mycenaean (1300-1100 BC), the 'dark age'

(1100-700), the 'archaic' (700-480), the 'classical' (480-322 BC) and the 'Hellenic (322-30 BC).[31] The Mycenaean period marked the beginning of the successive waves of migration and occupation. The Mycenaeans (also known as the Achaeans) were people from the southern part of the mainland, who migrated to many parts of what is now southern Greece. They established a prosperous and vibrant society, which was heavily influenced by the Minoan culture. In Crete, this period coincided with the end of the Minoan era. As I have already mentioned, the Myceneans took over control of Knossos and spread their influence over much of the island. The second quotation at the beginning of this section, which is from Homer's epic poem *The Odyssey*, gives some idea of Crete's prosperity at this time. No one knows when *The Odyssey* (or Homer's other classic work, *The Iliad*) was written or how much of it was based on real events. In fact, no-one knows who Homer really was or even if he existed at all; it is possible that the poems were the work of several different people. This is an obvious case where 'history' and 'myth' are inextricably intertwined. However, it seems fairly safe to assume that these and other references to Crete refer to the Mycenaean era.[32]

The Mycenaean period appears to have been followed by several centuries of economic and cultural stagnation. In Crete, this was the time when the next wave of Greek migration took place. The migrants, known as Dorians, came from the western part of the mainland. They appear to have been more war-like than the Mycenaeans and many of the indigenous Cretans fled to the interior of the island. According to Rackham and Moody, the population of Crete decreased during this period, agricultural production declined and 'writing became a lost or rare art'.[33] The Dorians dominated Crete for the next ten centuries, until the Roman invasion, and the period as a whole is often referred to in Crete as the Doric era. Over the years, there was a gradual mixing of peoples and cultures. As Detorakis says, 'Minoans, Mycenaeans and Dorians in Crete now merged together to form a new ethnic and cultural identity'.[34]

The archaic and classical periods are those for which ancient Greece is most renowned. This is the time when the city states were at their height, science, art and culture flourished and Greek influence spread far afield. However, it was also a time of conflict, including wars between the various cities and with neighbouring powers. The classical period is particularly significant. It begins at the time when Athens was in its heyday and ends with the rise of Alexander the Great, who waged the wars that extended the Greek empire beyond the eastern Mediterranean to Persia, central Asia and Egypt. This period is well portrayed by the historical novelist, Mary Renault., who wrote many books about life in classical Greece, including three about Alexander the Great.[35]

In Crete, the Dorian Greeks also established city states. The term 'city' is somewhat misleading. The Greek word, πόλης, means town as well as city and, as Rackham and Moody point out, those in Crete were more like large villages.[36] Crete's city states also seem to have lacked much of the social and cultural sophistication of those on the mainland and there is little sign of the democratic governance for which ancient Athens is so renowned. The Cretan system of governance appears to have been modelled on that of Sparta, with which there were close ties, rather than Athens.[37] According to Makrakis, under the Dorians, 'Crete went from being a patriarchal kingdom to an oligarchic and aristocratic organisation'.[38] However, Crete's cities appear to have had remarkably well-developed legal systems. The main evidence for this is the inscription of an elaborate code of law found at the site of the city of Gortyn. This code, which is thought to date back to 480-460 BC, is the oldest surviving written code of law in Europe. It is in many respects comparable with Magna Carta, but even more incredible in that it was written sixteen centuries earlier.[39]

The Cretan cities were involved in many conflicts, both with each other and with neighbouring states. They were frequently caught up in the many wars raging in the region and the island was often divided, with some cities supporting one side and some another. This was, as we shall see, to become a common phenomenon. On the positive side, however the island's population had developed a reputation as good seamen and soldiers. Cretans had themselves begun to migrate to other parts of the Mediterranean, including Sicily, Etruria and Marseilles,[40] and they were often employed as soldiers and mercenaries. One of Alexander the Great's generals, Nearchus, was from Crete.

The death of Alexander in 323 BC marks the end of the classical period. The next three centuries, which are known as the Hellenic era, were a time of political chaos, but also one of economic prosperity and cultural achievement. The Greek empire gradually disintegrated, wars broke out between the various parts and anarchy often prevailed. However, in many areas trade and commerce continued to thrive and art and culture to flourish.

During this period Crete developed a reputation for warmongering and piracy. The wars between the city states and with neighbouring powers intensified and the island became known as a refuge for pirates. However, this reputation may be unfair. Because of its strategic location, Crete inevitably became a pawn in the many wars between the rival Hellenic states; because of its relative success in trade and commerce it was bound to become involved in the piracy that had largely replaced legal trade in the eastern Mediterranean; and because of the lack of alternative income-earning opportunities, its population was driven to become pirates and mercenaries. Moreover, it suffered as a result. Much of western Crete fell under the control of the Ptolemaeic dynasty of Egypt for many years, while the eastern part of the island was controlled by Rhodes following Crete's defeat in the 'Cretan War' of 205-201 BC. This war was, incidentally, really a war between Macedonia and Rhodes in which Crete happened to become involved.[41]

The number of city-states in Crete is not known and probably varied over time, but there appear to have been at least fifty.[42] Many of them were built on the sites of former Minoan towns.

The main ones are thought to have been Kydonia (now Chania) in the west, Lyttos (inland from the present resort of Hersonnissos) and Knossos in the north, and Phaistos and Gortyn, both in the fertile Mesara Plain in the south. However, there are few visible remains of this era on these sites. One reason for this is that they were subsequently occupied and rebuilt by later conquerors, such as the Romans and Venetians. The location of Cretan towns is a good example of the curious mixture of continuity and change in the island's history. Although the towns have been rebuilt and the names often changed, the same sites have been used by successive waves of civilisation.

There were two important Dorian cities in the Aghios Nikolaos area. One was Lato, which was located in the hills a few kilometres inland from Aghios Nikolaos. It was formerly a Minoan site, but was not redeveloped by subsequent invaders. Consequently, the remains of the Doric buildings are still clearly visible. It is generally regarded as the best-preserved Doric site in Crete. Its location is even more spectacular than that of Gournia, with magnificent views both to the coast and inland. The town flourished between the 7th and 3rd centuries BC, ruling over a large territory, including the small port of Kamara, which is all that then existed of the present settlement of Aghios Nikolaos. Alexander the Great's general, Nearchus, is believed to have come from Lato.[43]

The other important city in the area was Olous, a coastal settlement near the present-day village of Elounda. Like Lato, it was located on the site of a former a Minoan town. It was an important city, playing a major role in maritime trade. According to Makrakis, there were border disputes between Lato and Olous, but towards the end of the period the two eventually signed a peace agreement.[44] Unfortunately, there is not much to be seen of Olous today because the sea level has risen and the remains of the town are submerged under water.

There was a gradual transition between the Greek and Roman periods. The first Roman invasion of Greece was in 146 BC but Athens was not taken until 86 BC. In Crete, the first invasion was a few years later, in 71 BC. This was repelled, but another attempt in 69 BC was successful and two years later the Romans controlled the whole island. This marked the end of the first period of major Greek influence in Crete. However, by this time there had been so much intermixing of Cretan and Greek peoples and culture that, as we shall see later, from this point onwards their histories are irrevocably linked.

Roman Crete

> The Romans never attempted to Latinise the island. In any case this would have been a vain undertaking, both because of the nature of the land and of the inhabitants. (Detorakis, 1994, p.88).

Crete came under Roman control at more or less the same time as Britain. While Julius Caesar was invading Britain, his rival Pompey the Great was consolidating Roman control over the eastern Mediterranean. His main mandate was to stop piracy, which was disrupting Roman trade. The invasion of Crete was prompted partly by the island's involvement in piracy but also by the fact that Cretan mercenaries were supporting Mithridates, king of the Black Sea state of Pontus, who rebelled against the Romans in 74 BC. The first attempt to invade the island, in 71 BC, was led by Marcus Antonius, father of the more famous Marcus Antonius otherwise known as Mark Anthony. It was made on the north coast, near present-day Iraklio. The second attempt, which was successful, was led by Quintus Caecilius Metellus, who was later given the name 'Creticus', in recognition of his success.[45] Metellus began his attack in the west, at Kydonia, and then moved gradually eastwards. The Cretans fought hard to repel Metellus' forces, but were eventually overcome. According to Makrakis, the last stronghold of Cretan resistance was the town of Ierapetra.[46]

Crete was occupied by the Romans for nearly 450 years. Again there are similarities with Britain, where Roman rule lasted for much the same length of time. In the early years, Crete was affected by the internal problems of the Roman Empire. This was the time when Mark Anthony and Octavius were competing for power. Both leaders used Crete as a means of gaining support and the island was divided, with some cities supporting one and some the other.[47] Once again, Crete found itself caught up in other people's wars.

However, the remaining 400 or so years of Roman rule were a time of relative peace and prosperity. The Romans established the first effective island-wide system of governance, building on a loose alliance of cities, known as the *koinon*, which was established during the Hellenic period but seldom operated very effectively because of the frequent conflicts between the cities. Their headquarters was the southern town of Gortyn. For much of the time, Crete and Cyrenaica (on the northern coast of Africa in what is now Libya), were governed as one province, and Gortyn was the provincial capital. They also built infrastructure (including roads, bridges and aqueducts) and promoted economic development. Crete was important to the Romans not only because of its strategic position but also because of it agricultural productivity. It became an important source of olive oil, wine and other produce.

Somewhat surprisingly, the Cretans do not seem to have made any serious attempt to overthrow the Romans. This was no doubt due partly to the economic prosperity. If the Cretans were doing well under Roman rule, they would have had little cause for complaint. Probably more important, however, was the fact that, as Detorakis suggests in the quotation at the beginning of this section, the Romans did not try to 'Latinise' the island. There is evidence of some cultural influence; for example, the worship of the Roman god Jupiter.[48] However, the Cretans appear to have retained most aspects of their own culture and, perhaps most importantly, their own language and script. In this respect, the situation was very different to that in Britain, where Roman culture appears to have had more impact, particularly on language.

Why didn't the Romans have more impact on Cretan culture? There are probably several reasons. Firstly, the number of Romans who actually lived there was relatively small and most of them were soldiers or administrators rather than settlers. There appears to have been some Roman migration, but not enough to have had a major impact on Cretan life or cause conflict with local people. It is interesting to compare this situation with that in the British Empire many centuries later. There was a major difference between those parts of the British Empire where there was widespread British settlement, notably North America, Australasia, Kenya and southern Africa, and those where the British were, like the Romans in Crete, merely administrators.

Secondly, when the Romans conquered Crete there was already a well-established society and culture, based on the many centuries of Minoan, Mycenaean and Doric influence. This was true not just in Crete but in the whole of what is now Greece. In fact, the Romans were probably far more influenced by the Greeks than vice versa. This may help to explain the difference in the impact of Roman occupation between Crete and Britain. Britain had never been exposed to any major 'civilisation' and so had relatively little social organisation or cultural development. Once again a comparison with the British Empire is relevant. The difference between Britain and Crete under the Romans is not unlike that between India and Africa under British rule. The Indian subcontinent was home to one of the oldest 'world civilisations', while in Africa the situation was much more like that in pre-Roman Britain. This difference affected both the way in which the British administered its African and Indian colonies and the long-term impact of British rule.

Thirdly, the establishment of Roman rule in Crete coincided with the establishment of Christianity. Christianity is believed to have reached Crete in 47 AD, when St Paul, on his way from Jerusalem to Rome, was forced by bad weather to land (some say he was shipwrecked) on the southwest coast. Paul did not stay long, but he left one of his disciples, Titus, to establish the Christian church on the island. According to Detorakis, it is not known whether Titus was Cretan or originated elsewhere.[49] However, Cretan or not, he became a legendary figure. He was the first bishop in Crete and later the island's patron saint and, due at least in part to his efforts, Christianity spread rapidly. By the third century AD, Christians were being martyred for their beliefs. The most famous were the ten saints (*Agii Deka*) of Gortyn, who became revered not just for their religious fervour but also for their patriotism. As Llewellyn Smith says, 'very early in Greek history these two virtues came to be connected, and even by some people identified with each other'.[50] The importance of this will emerge later. We shall see that Christianity has played a critical role in determining not just the course of events in subsequent historical eras but also Cretan culture and identity today.

The other possible reason why the Romans had relatively little impact on Cretan culture is that, as the opening quotation from Detorakis suggests, if they had tried, it would have been 'a vain undertaking', because of 'the nature of the land and of the inhabitants.' Although he does not elaborate, the implications are clear. Firstly, Crete's rugged terrain would have made it difficult to effectively 'Latinise' the whole island. And secondly, the people would have resisted any attempt to undermine their culture or do things against their will. The early Christian martyrs are a poignant reminder of this. Many of the northern European tribes, including the Britons, had a reputation for being difficult to govern, but the recalcitrant Cretans must have been just as bad.

There is relatively little physical evidence of the Roman era in Crete. There were Roman settlements all over the island, including Olous and Kamara in the Aghios Nikolaos area, and archaeologists have found relics of Roman occupation in many places.

However, the only well preserved Roman town is the provincial capital, Gortyn. Gortyn (also known as Gortys) is a fascinating archaeological site because there are relics of both the Greek and Roman eras. Moreover, the juxtaposition of the two architectural styles shows how the buildings of one era formed the basis for those of the next. For example, the inscription of the Dorian code of law for which Gortyn is famous was found on the wall of a Roman building.

The transition from the Roman era to the Byzantine was, like so many phases of Cretan history, a gradual one. In the Byzantine Museum in Athens, the term 'mutate' is used to describe this transition. During the latter part of the Roman era, the balance of power within the Roman Empire gradually shifted from Rome to the eastern Mediterranean. There were two critical dates. The first was 325 AD, when the emperor Constantine the Great moved the capital to Byzantium, an old Greek city at the mouth of the Black Sea, and renamed it Constantinople. The second was 395 AD, when, seventy years later, the emperor Theodosius divided the empire into two parts, west and east. The west was governed from Rome and the east from Constantinople. In the west, the empire rapidly disintegrated and there followed a long period of relative economic and cultural stagnation and political turmoil. In Britain, this is often referred to as the 'dark ages'. But the eastern, or Byzantine, part of the Empire thrived for more than a thousand years.

Byzantine Crete

> The Byzantine civilisation is a synthesis of the ancient Greek culture and language, with the spirit of the Roman administration, plus the Christian religion, the Orthodox faith. (Economides, I., *The Two Faces of Greece*, Athens, 1992, p.73)

As the above quotation suggests, the Byzantine Empire is a strange phenomenon. It was an extension of the Roman Empire, but for most of the period Greek was the national language and Orthodox Christianity the dominant religion. And its capital, Constantinople, was later to become the capital of the Turkish Empire, which became the greatest enemy of the Greeks and of Christianity. The effects of this confusion are still evident today, in that Istanbul (as Constantinople is now called), although in Turkey, is still the headquarters of the Greek Orthodox Church – and the Greeks persist in calling it Constantinople (*Κωνσταντινούπολη* in Greek).

There is very little information on the Byzantine era in Crete. This is somewhat surprising, not just because it lasted for a long time, but also because on the mainland it is regarded as a very important period. Irene Economides, the author of the above quotation, describes it as 'a civilisation of great nobility and fineness, which covered all the branches of knowledge' and quotes a professor of Byzantine art as saying that 'if ancient Greece expressed the "beautiful", Byzantine Greece expressed the "sublime"'.[51] The reason for the paucity of information seems to be partly a lack of archaeological evidence but primarily the fact that Crete was again on the margins of the empire and so attracted little attention from historians of the day.

The Byzantine era in Crete is conventionally divided into three parts, of which only two are actually periods of Byzantine rule. The first part covers the period from 324-824 AD. According to Detorakis, this appears to have been a time of relative peace and possibly agricultural prosperity. The administrative system established under the Romans continued to function and Gortyn remained the capital. However, there were many natural disasters, including earthquakes and outbreaks of the plague, and periodic attempts to invade the island, including one by Slavs in 623.[52]

The 'first Byzantine' period came to an end in 824, when Arabs took control of the island. The Arabs were Moors (also known as Saracens) from Cordoba, one of many small Moslem states in Spain at the time. Driven out of Spain by inter-state conflicts, they made their way eastwards, settling first in Egypt and then in Crete. They survived through raiding and piracy. They landed on the north coast and established their headquarters at Chandax, on the site of present-day Iraklio, from which they controlled the island for the next 137 years.

Historians seem to differ both on the Arabs' reasons for settling in Crete and on the nature and extent of their influence. Some claim that they deliberately targeted Crete, that they controlled the whole of the island and that large numbers of Cretans were forced to convert to Islam. But others suggest that they merely used Crete as a convenient place from which to conduct raids elsewhere, that they only occupied the northern coastal area and that there were relatively few converts. However, whatever the real situation was, the period of Arab rule is generally regarded as a 'dark age', if only for the lack of information.[53]

The rulers of the Byzantine Empire were concerned at the loss of Crete, partly because it represented a diminution of their power but also because of its strategic position on the trade routes of the eastern Mediterranean. They made several unsuccessful attempts to regain it, but in 961 AD, after a long siege, they finally took control of Chandax.

The 'second Byzantine' period was shorter than the first. The Byzantine rulers made a major effort to strengthen their hold on the island during this period. They built fortifications, re-established the former administrative system - this time with the headquarters at Chandax, and revived the Christian church. They also granted large areas of land to some influential leaders, thereby promoting the development not only of a landowning class but also of a political system based on the patronage of a small number of powerful families – a system that, as we shall see later, continues to exist today. According to Detorakis, there was a widely-held belief that some of these landowners were settlers introduced by the emperor Alexis I. Kommenos to strengthen his control, but this has not been historically proven.[54] It appears to be another case where it is difficult to separate history and myth.

Religion played a very important role during the whole of the Byzantine era. Large numbers of churches were built and most of the art for which the Byzantine era on mainland Greece is renowned was religious in nature. The relatively few relics that exist of this period in Crete are of churches and religious art. There are three interesting examples in the Aghios Nikolaos area. One is a mosaic from a small church dating back to the first Byzantine period, which is located near the site of the drowned city of Olous. Both Olous and Kamara appear to have thrived during the first Byzantine period, but there is no record of them in the second.[55] Another is the little church of Aghios Nikolaos, from which the town got its name, which was built during the second Byzantine period. It is located a short distance north of the present town, on the road to Elounda, and although now in the grounds of a large hotel, is open to the public. The third site is the church of Panagia Kera, near the village of Kritsa, which was originally built in the second Byzantine period and then extended during the Venetian era and is renowned for its frescoes.

However, this was also a period of conflict within the Christian church. The conflicts were ostensibly over doctrinal issues, but they also reflected the struggle for power between Rome and Constantinople. During the 8th and 9th centuries, the main doctrinal issue was the use of icons, which were condemned by the church in Constantinople but not that in Rome. According to Detorakis, the Cretans, although falling under Constantinople, supported the use of icons.[56] Another major issue was the relative importance of the three components of the Trinity (Father, Son and Holy Ghost). It was reputedly a unilateral decision by the Pope to include a reference to the Son in the Nicene code that finally precipitated a formal split between the two churches in 1054. This split, known as the Great Schism, marks the separation of what are now known as the Catholic and Orthodox Churches.

There is little evidence of Cretan resistance either to the Byzantine rulers or to the Arabs. The lack of resistance to the Byzantines is not surprising, since the Byzantine Empire was both Greek and Christian and by this time Crete was in many respects Greek and undoubtedly Christian. However, the apparent lack of resistance to Arab rule is more surprising. Detorakis considers two possible reasons - the possibility that Arab influence was not as widespread as some people thought and the disagreement between the Cretans and the Byzantines over the use of icons – but finds neither convincing.[57] There appears to be insufficient information to draw any conclusions, or even to be sure that there was little resistance, either then or during the two Byzantine periods.

The end of Byzantine rule in Crete was the result of two interrelated power struggles: the religious-based conflicts between Rome and Constantinople and internal rivalries within the Byzantine Empire. The last two centuries of the Byzantine era was the time of the Crusades. Although these Crusades were directed primarily against the Turks, they were complicated by the divisions within the Christian church. In 1203 the Fourth Crusade turned its attention from the Holy Land to Constantinople and the following year the city was taken and the Byzantine Empire collapsed. The leader of the Crusade, Boniface of Montferrat (a territory in northern Italy) was assisted in this venture by the son of a former Byzantine emperor, Isaac II Angelos, who had been deposed by his brother a few years earlier. The alliance included a deal whereby Angelos would be restored to power and in return Boniface would be given Crete. The deal was honoured, but apparently Boniface had his hands full with the other territories that he gained, particularly Thessaloniki, and so sold Crete to Venice 'for the meagre price of 1000 silver marks (about 5000 gold ducats)'.[58]

Venetian Crete

> It was under the Venetians that Crete saw an artistic and literary renaissance that was unique in the Greek world.

> ...Crete became a liability, to be retained only at exces-
> sive cost in arms and blood. But she was a symbol. With
> her loss would go not only the wines, silks and oils of the
> island itself, not only the valuable spices of Alexandria,
> but also the hope of a Hellenic-Latin culture in the Aege-
> an - the last outpost of art and learning and literature set
> amid the encroaching barbarism of the Ottoman Turks.
> Europe knew this. (Llewellyn Smith, 2007, pp.24, 26)

There is much more information about the Venetian period than
the Roman or Byzantine. There are three main reasons for this.
The first one is simply that it is more recent and so historical
records are better. The second is that there is more physical evidence, especially in the form of buildings and infrastructure,
such as forts and harbours. The third, and perhaps most important, reason is that, as the above quotation suggests, Crete's role
in European history became critical during this period.

In 1204 the histories of Crete and Greece temporarily parted
ways. When Constantinople collapsed and Crete was ceded to
Venice, the rest of what is now Greece was divided up between
various western European (referred to by the Greeks as 'Frank-
ish') powers. In 1261 the Byzantines reconquered Constantinople and much of the country was reunited under Byzantine rule.
This third Byzantine era lasted until 1453, when Constantinople
was conquered again, this time by the Turks, and Greece became
part of the Turkish Empire. But Crete remained under Venetian
control throughout this period. There was no third Byzantine era
and the island was not conquered by the Turks until 1669.

However, although there was no longer a political link with
Greece, Greek influence remained strong and during the latter
part of the period, after the fall of Constantinople in 1453, Crete's
role became critical. Llewellyn Smith quotes an anonymous poet
who tells how, when the city fell, the then emperor, Constantine
XII, told his followers to cut off his head and take it to Crete. According to Llewellyn Smith, this was a signal that it was now up

to Crete to preserve and foster Greek culture.[59] And this in fact is what happened. Some Greek scholars and artists had already come to Crete and after 1453 'what had been a trickle became a stream'.[60] Some stayed there, but others used it as a stepping stone to move further west, to Italy and France, taking Greek culture with them.

Historians differ in their assessment of the Venetian era. Some, such as Makrakis and (albeit to a lesser extent) Detorakis, emphasise the negative aspects, such as the number of Venetian settlers, the establishment of a Venetian ruling class, the high rates of taxation and, in particular, the attempts to crush the Orthodox Church and replace it with the Catholic. However others, such as Llewellyn Smith, focus on the positive aspects, especially the flourishing of art and culture.

There is evidence to support both perspectives. On the positive side, it appears that the various attempts by the Venetians to subvert the local culture and religion largely failed. Greek remained the main language, even for official purposes, and (due in large part to the role of the monasteries) the Orthodox Church continued to survive. Moreover, although there were large numbers of Venetian settlers, many became integrated into the local society. There was much intermarriage, some converted to the Orthodox faith and, as Detorakis concedes, even those 'who remained Catholic, began to feel more Greek than Venetian'.[61]

The cultural evidence is also irrefutable. Crete was not just a refuge for the culture of Byzantine Greece. During the sixteenth century it became the focus of a two-way cultural exchange between East and West. This was the time of the renaissance in western Europe and, due in large part to the role of Crete, Byzantine art had a significant influence on that in the west. For a brief period, Crete was again at the centre of civilisation, rather than on the periphery. This is reflected in a number of ways. For example, in the Byzantine Museum in Athens, there are several rooms devoted to Crete's role at this time, while Llewellyn Smith calls this period the 'Cretan Renaissance' and Detorakis refers to 'the Cretan School of art'. Moreover, one of Crete's most famous sons, the painter El Greco, was a product of this era. His real name was Domenikos Theotokopoulos, but he moved to Italy, where he became known as El Greco (the Greek).

However, the many Cretan revolts during the Venetian era support the claims that, especially in the period before the fall of Constantinople, it was also a time of hardship and oppression for many of the local people. According to Detorakis, there were at least 27 uprisings of one sort or another, the first in 1211, soon after the Venetians took control, and the last in 1527. Many of the revolts started in the southwest, in a mountainous area called Sphakia, which had been a refuge for Cretans since the end of the Minoan era and has a long reputation for resisting every occupying force. Another major centre was the Lasithi Plateau, whose location and history was in many ways similar to that of Sphakia. According to Rackham and Moody, in 1343 the Venetians banned any settlement or cultivation on the plateau in an attempt to curb rebel activity.[62]

Detorakis describes these revolts as a mixture of 'national' and 'social' movements.[63] However, I suspect they were also personal struggles for power. In many cases, the leaders appear to have been members of the prominent landowning families established during the second Byzantine era and, since they lost much of their power to the local Venetian aristocracy, they probably bore the biggest grudge against the Venetians. There were apparently many conflicts between these local leaders as well as between them and the Venetians. The outcomes of these revolts were mixed. Those involved were often severely punished, but in some cases they resulted in concessions to the local population.

The most impressive relics of the Venetian era are the harbours and forts. There are three main harbours: Chania, Rethymno and Iraklio. They are impressive not just because of their historical interest but also because of their aesthetic value. Those at Chania and Rethymno are particularly attractive because the modern towns have been built around them. Chania and Rethymno also have two of the most impressive Venetian forts (or *fortezza*, as the Venetians called them). In both cases, the old parts of the town nestle under the walls of the *fortezza*. They are fascinating areas to explore. However, there are remains of Venetian forts in many other towns, including Ierapetra and Sitia in the eastern part of the island.

Although, according to Makrakis, Agios Nikolaos was established during the Venetian era,[64] there are no signs of a Venetian harbour or fort. Presumably the town was very small in those days. However, a few kilometres north of Agios Nikolaos, the small rocky island of Spinalonga is home to one of the most notable Venetian forts. Spinalonga lies just off the coast of Elounda, near the site of the old submerged city of Olous. During the Venetian era, the Olous site became an important salt-producing area; a role which it retained until the 1970s. Because of its strategic location at the northern end of the Gulf of Mirabella (so named incidentally by the Venetians) and the entrance to the sheltered inlet that led to Olous, there had been fortifications at Spinalonga from Minoan times. The Venetian fort was built between 1579 and 1586, during the latter part of Venetian rule.[65] It is an impressive edifice and, as we shall see later, represents only one part of the little island's fascinating history. According to Makrakis, there was also a Venetian lookout on a hill overlooking my local beach, Almyros, though I have yet to discover its exact location.[66]

The impressive harbours and forts testify to the fact that the Venetians were a seafaring nation and that their main interest in Crete was to control the trade routes in the Eastern Mediterranean. Their hold on the island was constantly threatened, not just by local uprisings, but also by external powers, including other western European states, Byzantines, Arabs and Turks. After the fall of Constantinople, the pressure from the Turks increased. In 1571, the Turks took control of Cyprus, leaving Crete as the last bastion of Venetian rule. This prompted the Venetians to strengthen their fortifications and build several new forts, including Spinalonga.

In 1645 the Turks invaded western Crete and took Chania. Despite resistance from both Venetians and Cretans, the Turks rapidly gained ground. By 1648 they had control of most of the island except the capital, Candia (present-day Iraklio). In 1650 they attacked Candia. However, it took them nearly 20 years to capture the city. During the siege the Venetians were supported by various western European powers. In 1669 the city finally fell, marking the end not just of the 25-year Cretan War (as it became known) but of Venetian rule in Crete. The Turks and Venetians signed a treaty, in which it was agreed that the Venetians would retain control of three forts: Souda and Gramvousa in the northwest and Spinalonga in the northeast. However, the treaty was not honoured, war broke out again and the three forts were eventually taken. The last to fall was Spinalonga, which held out until 1715.

Turkish Crete

Alas poor Cretans! Where are your horses and where are your mules? Where are your hounds, and where are your hawks? Where are your thoughts and where are your lofty houses? Where are your scribes? (Quotation from Marinos Tzane Bouniales, Cretan poet 1620-85, in Historical Museum of Crete, Iraklio)

The history of Crete under the Turks is the history of her revolts. (Llewellyn Smith, 2007, p.80)

One of the most interesting aspects of the history of the Turkish era, for me anyway, is the way in which it is portrayed. Not only in Crete but in Greece as a whole, one gets the feeling that people are trying to shut this period out of their memories, much as one would a bad dream. For example, as far as I know, there is no museum in Greece about the Turkish era. There is a museum in

Thessaloniki's famous White Tower, which was a Turkish prison, but I was disappointed to find nothing in it about the Turkish period. It is said that the Tower's name and its symbolism stem from the fact that one of the prisoners whitewashed it in return for his release. And in Crete, Iraklio's otherwise excellent History Museum has very little material on this period in the island's history.

Furthermore, most references to the Turkish occupation are negative. The only positive references are to the various acts of resistance. For example, a display board in Thessaloniki's Byzantine Museum claims that the Turkish conquest led to 'tremendous democratic decline, incalculable material destruction and four centuries of intellectual, social and economic backwardness'. The only positive aspect, it says, was that it 'did much to restore the cohesion of the Greek world'. The quotation from Llewellyn Smith at the beginning of this section can be interpreted in two ways. The most obvious interpretation is that there were many revolts under Turkish rule. However, the less obvious one is that historians of the period tend to give far more attention to the revolts than to anything else.

Detorakis' *History of Crete* is no exception. The author deserves much credit for providing a very detailed account of all aspects of the Turkish era. However, even he paints a generally negative picture of everything except the Cretan revolts. In fact, he maintains that Turkish rule was in many respects, including the large numbers of Turkish immigrants, the high rates of taxation and the violence of the *janissaries* (the Turkish soldiers), worse than that on the Greek mainland.[67] The general impression one gets about this era is that (to parody the words of the professor of Byzantine art quoted earlier) if the Venetian era was bad, then the Turkish era was hell.

Were things really so bad? Foreign writers, such as Llewellyn Smith and Rackham and Moody, suggest that, as in the Venetian era, there were positive as well as negative aspects of Turkish rule.[68] Economically, for example, after an initial period of de-population and economic decline (inevitable after so many years of war), Crete once again became a prosperous agricultural and trading society. One of the main trading centres was the little island of Spinalonga, which was taken over by the Turks after the eventual Venetian defeat and by 1881 had a population of over 1,000.[69] Remains of many of the Turkish buildings can still be seen.

Socially and politically, the picture is similar. There were large numbers of Turkish immigrants; however, like their Venetian predecessors, many were gradually assimilated into the local community. As Detorakis himself points out, almost all the immigrants were men, so intermarriage was common.[70] There is no doubt that the population was heavily taxed, probably more so than under the Venetians. However, taxation itself was nothing new, having been employed by all previous regimes. Moreover, a system of compulsory labour introduced by the Venetians was apparently seldom used by the Turks.[71] Similarly, any attempt at resistance was severely punished, but this was also the case during the Venetian era. One of the worst practices was the abduction of children, the boys to be trained as *janissaries* and the girls to serve in harems. However, through this system many Cretans rose to positions of authority in the Ottoman Empire. Two Sultans were apparently half-Cretan and two Sultanas fully Cretan.[72]

The Turks approach to religion is particularly interesting. On the positive side, they formally reinstated the Orthodox Church. But on the negative side, they used the Church as an instrument for controlling the people and taxed it heavily. Moreover, although Christianity was tolerated, Christians were regarded as second class citizens. They were treated more harshly in courts of law and, most importantly, taxed far more heavily. Apparently, many Cretans converted to Islam for practical reasons. However, since many people converted in name only and there were many families and villages where some people converted but others did not, this actually helped to foster good relations between the two communities. This juxtaposition of the two religions is also reflected in the architecture. For example, in Rethymno's *fortez-za*, which like most of the Venetian forts was taken over by the Turks, there is a mosque that was built on the site of a former Catholic church and, a hundred or so metres away, an Orthodox Christian church.

In the case of culture, the positive side is less obvious. The Turks were not interested in promoting art and culture and the only schools they encouraged were the religious *madrasa*. Hence, the frequent reference to this era as a 'dark age'. However, during the latter part of the period, the situation began to improve. Greek, which had survived as the main language for general communication, was reinstated as the official language in 1868, the education system was revived, libraries and newspapers began to appear and Cretan literature to emerge.[73]

Whatever the pros and cons of Turkish rule, there is no doubt that there was much resentment among the Cretans. This is reflected in the large number of revolts that arose during the latter part of the period. These revolts were in many respects similar to those under the Venetians, in that they occurred sporadically and were led by prominent Cretan families. However, they were more complex and potentially more powerful because they were linked to anti-Turkish activities elsewhere, particularly the struggle for independence in mainland Greece but also the wider conflicts in the Mediterranean as a whole.

As in Venetian times, the two mountain strongholds, Sphakia and the Lasithi Plateau, were the centres of many of these revolts. As Detorakis says, 'Lasithi was to eastern Crete what Sphakia was to western Crete: the base and supply point of the rebels'.[74] Lack of coordination between the various uprisings was again a problem. According to Detorakis, there were various attempts to establish an island-wide organisation, but they lacked any overall leadership.

Although there were a number of earlier uprisings (the most prominent being in Sphakia in 1770), the first major period of revolt was between 1821 and 1830. It was prompted by the Greek war of independence, which began on 25 March 1821, when Greece declared itself independent. Although independence was not actually achieved until 1830, this date is always regarded as Greece's independence day and commemorated annually throughout the country. The Cretans not only staged their own revolts but also fought on the mainland. Their leaders apparently hoped that, if the Greeks succeeded, Crete would become part of an independent Greece. The Greeks were eventually successful, but Crete was not included in the new Greek state. The latter's boundaries were actually very limited, excluding much of what is now northern Greece and many of the Aegean islands. According to Detorakis, Crete's exclusion was 'due to British diplomacy'.[75] The island was instead given to Turkey's ally, Egypt, which had helped the Turks to suppress the revolts in Crete.

The next seventy years in Crete were a time of political chaos and consequent economic decline. The second period of Egyptian rule (the first having been under the Ptolemies in the 3rd Century BC) lasted ten years. In 1840, following conflicts between the Egyptians and the Turks, a new international treaty was signed and Turkish rule was reinstated. The new Turkish administration, which moved its capital from Iraklio to Chania, was apparently more lenient, particularly in its attitude to Christians. However, by this time, the Cretan leaders were determined to oust the Turks and the island's future had become an international issue, involving many western European nations, especially Britain, France, Italy and Russia, who became known in history as the four 'Great Powers'. Both within Crete and outside, there were two schools of thought, one favouring unity with Greece and the other some form of Cretan autonomy under international supervision. The former appears, for reasons that I will explain later, to have been the preferred solution in Crete.

In 1866 the so-called Great Rebellion began. It was eventually quelled, but only after a great deal of violence and bloodshed, including the deaths of hundreds of Cretans in the Arkadi Monastery near Rethymno, who chose to sacrifice themselves rather than be captured by the Turks. Since the Cretans had managed to gain control of much of the island, the Turks were forced to enact a law (the Organic Act of 1868), which granted various concessions to the local population, including the establishment of Greek as the official language. However, according to Detorakis, the Act was weak and frequently violated.[76] Consequently, there were further uprisings in 1878, 1889, 1895 and 1897. Crete's most famous writer, Nikos Kazantzakis, was born in 1883, at the height of these final struggles against Turkish rule. His book, *Captain Michalis* (published in English as *Freedom and Death*),[77] provides a vivid picture of this period in Crete's history.

The Cretans were not the only people to challenge the Turks at this time. There were two other regional wars against the Turks: the Russian-Turkish war in 1877, which was won by the Russians, and the Greek-Turkish war in 1897, which the Turks won. It was the outcome of these two wars that finally led to the resolution, at least for the time being, of the 'Cretan question'. Turkey was forced to relinquish its control but the island became an international protectorate rather than a part of Greece.

Autonomous Crete

> The Cretan dream of union with Greece had proved to be illusory for yet another time. The leaders of the Cretan uprising were obliged to accept the solution of autonomy. (Detorakis, 1994, p.366)

> 'Lord, let my paradise be a Crete decked with myrtle and flags and let the minute when Prince George set foot on Cretan soil last for centuries.' (Zorba, in Kazantzakis, N., *Zorba the Greek*, 1961, p.26)

The first of the above quotations explains a lot about this period. Autonomy appears to have been regarded as a second-best option; Cretans would have preferred unity with Greece. I use the word 'appears' because, as with so many other issues in the island's history, we do not know what the majority of ordinary Cretans thought. We know from Greek historians, such as Detorakis and Makrakis, that this was what the resistance leaders wanted, but these historians tend not to question the desirability of Crete's unity with Greece. The second quotation, from Kazantzakis' novel *Zorba the Greek*, which is set in Crete during this period, suggests that at least some people thought otherwise.

At first sight, it may seem strange that even the leaders would prefer to be part of Greece than to be independent. When I learned that for fifteen years Crete had been a separate political entity with its own elected government, my immediate reaction was to ask why it had not remained so. One might have expected such an independently-minded people to welcome such a move. This was the first time they had been in control of their own affairs since Minoan times and the first time they had been able to elect their own leaders.

However, when one considers the historical background, it is easier to understand the desire for unity with Greece, especially but not only among the island's leaders. We have seen in the earlier sections of this chapter how, very early in its history, the island's people and its culture became inextricably linked with those of the mainland. This sense of unity is graphically expressed by Captain Michalis, the principal character in Kazantzakis' novel *Freedom and Death*, who comments to a friend after an earthquake: "An earthquake, Bertodulos, is nothing. Crete is a living thing. It's moving. One day you'll see the way it'll join with Greece." And we shall see, both in this section and in later chapters, how this attitude has affected its recent history.

Three other factors also help to explain the attitude to autonomy. Firstly, although the island was self-governing, it was not fully independent. As an international protectorate, it was under the supervision of the four Great Powers and, perhaps more importantly, it was still nominally under Turkish suzerainty. Consequently, the political battles that (as we shall see) continued during the fifteen years of autonomy were regarded as struggles not just for unity with Greece, but also for total liberation from external powers, especially the Turks. Secondly, Greece was still fighting to regain control of other parts of the Greek-speaking world and Crete was seen as part of that fight. And thirdly, these battles were, of course, also struggles for power between individual leaders.

During the period of autonomy, Crete had its own government, composed of a mixture of elected and appointed representatives and including both Christians and Moslems. It also had its own administrative and judicial system, and even its own currency. However, since it was a protectorate, it had a high commissioner, appointed by the Great Powers. The first high commissioner was Prince George of Greece, son of King George I of Greece (and, incidentally, uncle to Prince Philip, husband of Queen Elizabeth II). Moreover, as already mentioned, the Great Powers played a supervisory role. They actually divided the island between them: the Italians were responsible for the Chania region, the Russians for Rethymno, the British for Iraklio, and the French for the eastern region of Lasithi.[78] They also controlled the police force, which was staffed mainly by Italians.

Although Crete was not fully independent, there were considerable achievements during this period, including the restoration of law and order, the construction of infrastructure and the establishment of education and health services. The island, which had been devastated by the many years of war and political chaos, began to return to a degree of normalcy and prosperity. One of the public health measures adopted during this period was the establishment in 1904 of a leper colony on Spinalonga Island. Leprosy had become rife and, since at that time there was no cure, isolation was regarded as the best way of dealing with the problem. Spinalonga was chosen because it was relatively inaccessible and, since most of the former Turkish inhabitants had left, virtually uninhabited. The lepers were accommodated in the buildings constructed and used by the Turks. This final stage in Spinalonga's history continued until 1957, by which time a cure had been found so the remaining patients were transferred to the mainland. During the period of autonomy, all the patients were from Crete; but later, after the union with Greece, there were also some from other parts of the country. .

This was also the time when archaeologists began to conduct detailed explorations of the Minoan sites. For example, Arthur Evans began work at Knossos in 1900 and Harriet Boyd, the archaeologist who unearthed Gournia, began her explorations in 1901. Evans had visited Knossos in 1894, but was not able to begin excavations until there was political stability on the island. These activities marked the beginning of a different sort of invasion: that of archaeologists and historians keen to explore the island's unique past. This invasion, which is still taking place today, has been generally beneficial, in that it has put Crete on the map and, as we shall see in the next chapter, contributed to the growth of its tourist industry. However, there has also been an element of exploitation, in that many 'outsiders' have gained fame through the exploration of the island's historical resources.

The generally positive achievements during this period were, however, marred by internal conflicts over the island's future. Some Cretans were content with the new autonomous government but others still wanted unification with Greece. The leader of the latter group was Eleftherios Venizelos, a prominent local politician, born in Chania, who was Minister of Justice in the Cretan government. The conflicts became highly personalised, with supporters of Prince George on one side and those of Venizelos on the other. In 1905, Venizelos resigned his position, led a revolt and established an alternative government in the hills outside Chania. The following year, there was an election, in which voters were divided: supporters of Prince George received 38,127 and those of Venizelos 33,279.[79]

In an attempt to resolve the issue, Prince George was removed and replaced by a former Greek prime minister, Alexandros Zaimis. However, the conflicts continued. In 1908, at the request of the Greek government which was being threatened by the Turks on its northern borders, the Cretan Assembly, apparently with substantial popular support, made a unilateral declaration of unity with Greece. The following year, Venizelos was invited to Athens as an advisor to the Greek government, and in 1910 he was elected to the Greek parliament and became prime minister. For the next three years, Crete was in a state of limbo. Although not officially part of Greece, it operated in many respects as if it was. The crux came with the Balkan Wars of 1912-13, when those Balkan states under Turkish rule, with help from Greece, overthrew the Turks. The Treaty of London, signed in May 1913, gave Greece control of Macedonia and the other parts of what is now northern Greece and most of the Aegean islands, including Crete. Thus on 1 December 1913, Crete officially became part of Greece.

One cannot help wondering what would have happened to Crete without Venizelos. Would other Cretan leaders have fought so persistently for unity and, if Venizelos had not become prime minister, would Greece have won the Balkan Wars and would Crete have been included in the Treaty of London? The island might well have remained autonomous much longer, or more likely (since less than a year after the unification with Greece, the First World War broke out) been occupied by yet another foreign power.

Unification with Greece

> The separate history of Crete essentially ended when it became politically united with mainland Greece. Following the date of its unification with Greece on 1 December 1913 it could not but share the same general

> history of the rest of Greece, of which it now comprised
> an organic part. (Detorakis, 1994, p.431)

The above quotation is taken from the last chapter of Detorakis' book. It is significant in that it reaffirms the widespread belief that Crete 'belongs in' Greece. Equally significant is the fact that he calls the chapter 'Liberated Crete'. However, for Detorakis, it was also a convenient way of avoiding the need to discuss this period in detail. This would have been difficult because it would have involved writing a history of modern Greece. I will follow his example. In this section I will merely give a brief summary of Greek history between 1913 and 1974, focusing on those events that involved or affected Crete. 1974 is a convenient point at which to end for two reasons. Firstly, it was the date when the democratic government that exists today was established. And secondly, it was around this time that Crete's next invasion began – and that is the subject of Part Two of the book.

The period between 1913 and 1974 was one of political turmoil in Greece, and thus often also in Crete. It was characterised by conflicts both within the country and outside. The internal conflicts were between alternative systems of government (democracy versus dictatorship, capitalist versus socialist) and between individual leaders, while the external ones included two world wars and an ongoing struggle against the Turks.

When Greece won its independence, it became a constitutional monarchy, with (like the UK) an elected parliament and a monarch as head of state. The first king was George I (father of Crete's Prince George). However, he was assassinated in 1913. He was replaced by his eldest son, Constantine, who happened to be married to the sister of Germany's leader, Kaiser Wilhelm. In the First World War, Greece sided with the allies, in part at least in the hope of gaining more territory (especially the hallowed city of Constantinople) from the Turks, who were allied with Germany. This created tensions between king and parliament and Constantine went into exile.

The end of the War marked the end of the Ottoman Empire. The 1920 Treaty of Sevres gave Greece a large expanse of territory, including the administration of the Smyrna area in what was then known as Asia Minor and a role in the transitional occupation of Constantinople. However, the government of the new state of Turkey, led by Mustafa Kemal Ataturk, refused to respect the terms of the treaty. This led to a war between Greece and Turkey, in which Greece was badly defeated and a new treaty agreed. The 1923 Treaty of Lausanne took away most of what Greece had gained under the earlier one. The Smyrna area became part of Turkey and Constantinople was renamed Istanbul.

Llewellyn Smith maintains that this defeat 'forced the Greeks to reassess not only their foreign policies but also their whole lives, their identity as a nation (as we would put it), their national destiny (as they would put it)'.[80] Furthermore, it also created a major humanitarian disaster, because the Treaty included provisions for a massive exchange of populations between Greece and Turkey. Approximately 1.3 million Christians living in Turkey were forced to move to Greece and nearly half a million Moslems living in Greece had to move to Turkey.

Meanwhile, King Constantine returned from exile after the War, but by this time the country was deeply divided between supporters of the monarchy and their republican opponents. The latter won and in 1924 the king was ousted and Greece became a republic. The next decade was a time of political turmoil, with numerous changes in government and attempted coups. Eventually, the monarchy was restored in 1935, with George II (grandson of George I) as king, and, a year later, with the King's support, parliament was abolished and an authoritarian regime under the dictator John Metaxas was established.

Crete played its part during this period. Eleftherios Venizelos, the Cretan politician who went on to become prime minister of Greece, is regarded as one of the country's most respected political leaders. He had two terms of office as prime minister (1910-20 and 1928-32) and, a staunch supporter of the republicans, at one time set up a rival government in Thessaloniki. According to Detorakis, Crete supported Venizelos during this time.[81] Other Cretan politicians also held positions in government, Cretan soldiers fought in the various wars, and in 1938 an attempted revolt against Metaxas was launched in Chania.

The island was also affected, albeit less than some parts of the country, by the 1923 exchange of Moslems and Christians between Turkey and Greece. About 30,000 Moslems were forced to leave Crete, and in their place about 34,000 Turkish Christians were settled there. In 2013, an interesting exhibition of local photographs from that time was held in Aghios Nikolaos. One of the organisers was a woman whose grandmother had been among the migrants. Meanwhile, in 1928 Elounda Bay acclaimed fame as one of the ports of call for the British Imperial Airways' flying boat service from London to Egypt and hence to India. According to Makrakis, there were eight flights a week to Egypt (Alexandria) and four to Bombay. The service continued until the outbreak of war in 1939.[82]

Greece entered the Second World War in March 1941, when Italy attacked its Albanian border. A few months earlier, on 28 October 1940, the Italians had issued an ultimatum to the Greeks to allow them to occupy the country but the Greek government had refused. This date is commemorated annually. It is known as Οχι day, since 'οχι' means 'no'. The initial attack by the Italians was repulsed but they were then attacked by the Germans and in less than three months the whole country was occupied.

The Germans invaded Crete on 20 May 1941. It was the last part of the country to be occupied. The allies had not expected Hitler to invade Crete: the Greek government had sought refuge there, the allied army had only a small force on the island, and most of the Cretan troops were on the mainland. However, despite the lack of preparation, the Germans met heavy resistance, not just from the small contingent of allied troops based on the island but also from the civilian population. The Germans eventually won and the whole island was occupied. However, the Battle of Crete, as it became known, is regarded as one of the most significant confrontations in the war. Several books have been written about it,[83] and it attracts a number of tourists to the island - including a friend of mine whose father was among the British troops involved.

The island was occupied by the Germans (and, in the eastern part, by the Italians) for four years. It was another period of hardship for the Cretans – and another period of resistance. Resistance groups were established all over the island. As in previous occupations, the mountains served as their base, and also as a refuge for the substantial number of allied troops stranded on the island. The various resistance efforts were, as in the past, inadequately uncoordinated. Moreover, they were also severely punished; the discovery of any attempt at sabotage led to mass executions. However, the constant harassment was effective, in that it forced the Germans to maintain forces on Crete that could have been more profitably utilised elsewhere.[84] One of the places most renowned for its resistance and most severely punished was Anogeia, a large village on the slopes of Mount Ida, southwest of Iraklio. Memories of the occupation are still strong in the village; photographs and other memorabilia can be seen in the village museum and in the *Kafeneio Michalos Skoulas* - one of the oldest coffee shops in Greece and now a popular café.

There was also fierce resistance on the mainland. In this case, however, it was complicated, and its impact hampered, by domestic politics. Most of the resistance forces were fighting for liberation not just from the Germans but also from their own authoritarian right-wing government. They saw themselves as nationalists and in many cases also as socialists or communists. The situation was further complicated by the fact that Britain and the other allied powers became involved in these disputes, in most cases on the side of the government, so the nationalists sometimes found themselves fighting the allies as well as the Germans.

It is therefore no surprise that, when the war ended and Greece was finally liberated from the Germans, it plunged straight into another war – this time, a civil war, which turned out also to be one of the first conflicts in the Cold War. The war, which lasted three years (1946-49) was between the official Greek government, supported by the British and the Americans, and the nationalists, who were supported by neighbouring Balkan countries who were now part of communist Eastern Europe. The nationalists were eventually defeated and the constitutional monarchy was reinstated.

There followed another period of political turmoil, with frequent changes in government and several attempted coups. Finally, in 1967, there was a successful coup, led by Colonel George Papadopoulos and condoned if not supported by the king, Constantine II. For the next eight years, Greece was ruled by a right-wing military junta. This was a period of relative stability and some economic progress, but also one of suppression. Dissenters, especially those of communist persuasion, were harshly punished, often with death, and consequently many people fled the country.

The 'Rule of the Colonels', as it is often known in Greece, came to an end in 1974, due partly to changes in the internal balance of power, but also to external events, notably the Turkish invasion of Cyprus, which had been a British territory from 1878 until 1960, when it became independent. Greece then entered a period of relative political stability. The monarchy was abolished, the country became a republic with an elected parliament and a president as head of state, and the Communist Party, which had been banned for many years, was allowed to operate legally. We shall see in the next chapter that, despite many ups and downs, this new democratic era has survived until today.

There is very little information, at least in English, about events in Crete during the post-war period. It appears to have been a time of relative peace and gradually increasing economic prosperity. It was also a time of population increase and change. In previous eras, there had been many fluctuations in population due to changes in economic conditions and outbreaks of war and disease, but the overall trend had been one of increase. In 1930 there were approximately 300,000 people, which is just over half the present number. By 1980, the number had increased to 400,000.[85]

Agriculture remained the main economic activity during this period and traditional customs and practices prevailed. Llewellyn Smith, who visited Crete in the early 1960s, described it as 'a society in a state of suspended animation'. He maintained that:

> The mountain songs still uphold the traditional heroic ideal of *levendia,* the gallant attitude to life. But the successive oppressors of the Cretans have gone and the songs now exist in a vacuum. For the first time in hundreds of years there is no enemy. The Cretan mountaineer is living in the past, but the twentieth century is beginning to catch up with him.'[86]

This probably explains why, as we shall see in the next chapter, Crete at this time became a popular place for hippies, who were to be its first tourists. For Cretans, however, life was still hard and many people left the island in search of employment.

Although the population remained predominantly rural during this period, the urban population began to increase. Rackham and Moody estimate that the rural population reached a peak of about 350,000 in 1950, and then began to decline.[87] Chania and Iraklio continued to be the main urban centres, but smaller towns also began to grow. Chania, which had been the capital since 1841, continued as such until 1971, when the seat of government was moved back to Iraklio.

One of the smaller towns that expanded rapidly during this period was Aghios Nikolaos. It had been growing in size and importance since the early 1900s, when the first road link to Neapoli was constructed and it became the headquarters of Lasithi province. However, at the end of the war its population was still little more than a thousand - less than that of Elounda. Its subsequent growth was encouraged by improvements in communication, including the construction of a road to Elounda in 1956 and the present road to Neapoli in 1968, and by the visit of a Greek film director, Nikos Koundouros, in 1961. The latter event led to the filming of a Walt Disney film, *The Moon-Spinners*, in the town in 1964 and, more significantly, the construction of a large tourist hotel, the Minos Beach, which opened the same year. The Minos Beach was not only the first major tourist hotel in Aghios Nikolaos but also one of the first in Crete. According to Makrakis, Aghios Nikolaos is 'the town from where Cretan tourism began'.[88]

To conclude this section, let us go back to Detorakis' assumption that Crete's unification with Greece in 1913 marked the end of its history as a separate entity. Is he right? Is Crete now destined to remain part of Greece and eventually become indistinguishable from the rest of the country? We will pursue this question in later chapters. However, the lessons of history suggest that it may not necessarily be the case. We have seen in this chapter that Cretan society has proved to be remarkably resilient. Despite successive invasions and occupations, the Cretan people have managed to retain a sense of identity and independence. Even after the unification with Greece this has been the case; Crete's role in the Second World War is the most obvious but not the only example.

Moreover, although Crete has been part of the Greek-speaking world for thousands of years, it has only been part of the modern Greek state for a hundred. This is a very short time in the history of any country. Scotland, for example, has been united with England for five hundred years, and yet it has retained a strong sense of national identity and in 2014 there was a referendum on its future political status, in which those in favour of remaining in the UK won, but only by a small margin.[89] And Crete's history goes back further than Scotland's. To borrow from the words of the Mother Superior quoted at the beginning of the chapter: What is a hundred years? Think of the Minoan civilisation that began 5,000 years ago and lasted for nearly 1,500 years!

Summary and Conclusion

This chapter has covered a period of more than 5,000 years. A brief summary may thus be useful, particularly for those readers who, for one reason or another, have not read the whole chapter. We began around 3,000 BC, when the Minoan civilisation for which Crete is so renowned began to emerge from the earlier stone-age cultures. The Minoan era lasted for about 1,500 years. We then saw how, towards the end of this period, the island began to be colonised by Greeks from the mainland, first the Mycenaeans and then the Dorians, and thus became part of the ancient Greek Empire. This process of colonisation had a major impact on the island; Cretans and mainland Greeks became so intermixed that by the first century BC their histories were irrevocably linked.

We then traced the successive invasions by peoples from further afield. The first were the Romans, who gradually conquered the Greek Empire and in 69 BC invaded and occupied Crete. The Romans ruled the island until the fourth century AD, when the Roman Empire began to disintegrate and the eastern part, which included Crete, evolved into the Byzantine Empire, with its capital in Constantinople. Then in 1204 the Byzantine Empire collapsed and Crete was given to the Venetians. The Venetian era was one of cultural and artistic achievement, but also one of hardship and oppression and the Cretan people frequently revolted against their rulers. Venetian rule came to an end in 1669, when the island was seized by the Turks and became part of the Ottoman Empire. The Turkish era is generally portrayed as one of cultural decline and extreme hardship and persecution and once again there were frequent Cretan revolts.

Finally, in the last part of the chapter, we saw how in 1897 the Turks were eventually expelled and Crete became an autonomous state under international protection, and then in 1913, due to pressure both from within Crete and from mainland Greece, the island was unified with Greece. And we looked briefly at the period following this unification, including Crete's occupation by the Germans and Italians during the Second World War. .

It is evident, even from this brief summary, that Crete's history is one of successive invasions by 'outsiders'. These invasions vary in many ways, not only in their origins, the way in which they occurred and their duration, but more importantly in the nature and extent of their impact and the way in which the Cretan people responded. There is in particular a significant difference between those involving mainland Greece and the others. Thus, the initial Greek colonisation had a much greater impact on the island than the later ones, while in the case of the unification with Greece the Cretans relinquished their sovereignty voluntarily.

However, there are also some common characteristics. These can be divided into three broad groups. The first group relate to the character of the invasions and their impact on Crete. Here four common features emerge clearly. Firstly, Crete's geography, particularly its strategic location and its resources, was a major factor behind most of the invasions. Secondly, the invasions were processes rather than events, evolving over time and often without clear beginnings and endings. Thirdly, they were multifaceted, affecting all aspects of the island, including its demography, its economy, its religion and culture, and its governance. And fourthly, in all cases there were both positive and negative impacts.

The second group relate to the Cretans' response. Here there are three main common characteristics. Firstly, the Cretan people (by which I mean those people living in and identifying with the island at that point in time) got what they could from the invasions. They exploited any economic and political opportunities that arose and adopted some social innovations and cultural practices. Consequently, Cretan society adapted and changed as a result of the invasions and in many cases Cretans benefited. Secondly, they nevertheless managed to retain their own social and cultural identity, including (except in the initial period of Greek colonisation) their language, and a sense of pride and self-esteem. And thirdly, they either ignored or resisted any aspects of the invasion that were not in their interests, resorting to violence if necessary.

The third set of common characteristics concern the implications for the invaders. In this case, there are two main points. Firstly, due to the island's sometimes hostile physical environment and the resilience of the Cretan people, it was not easy for them to maintain control of the island, especially the more remote parts. Secondly, due to the resilience of Cretan culture, it was not easy for them to integrate into the local society. Integration did take place but it took time and it was usually on Cretan terms, in the sense that the outsiders had to adopt the local language and often also the religion and customs.

With these points in mind, it is time now to move on to Part Two and explore what I have called the current invasion. There are three chapters in Part Two, corresponding to the three sets of conclusions outlined above. Chapter 4 describes the main features of the invasion, Chapter 5 looks at the Cretan response and Chapter 6 discusses the position of outsiders.

PART TWO

CRETE TODAY

Chapter 4

The Latest Invasion: Cosmopolitan Crete

There is no such thing as a Cretan race. Crete has always been cosmopolitan.
(Rackham, O. and J. Moody, *The Making of the Cretan Landscape*, Manchester University Press, 1996, p.88)

I live in a small block of twelve apartments on the outskirts of the town of Aghios Nikolaos. The apartments were originally built for short-term holiday lets. However, when the 2008 European financial crisis hit Greece, the owner, a local Greek businessman, decided to sell the apartments. Eight have been sold. Since the apartments are small, some people have bought two adjacent ones. Two have been bought by a French couple, two by a Serbian couple and two by an Englishman. They are used as holiday homes. The owners usually spend four to six months a year here. The seventh apartment is owned by a Greek man who is currently living in Belgium. His brother, who lives locally, looks after it for him. The eighth apartment is mine. The other four apartments have not yet been sold. One is rented to a young Romanian couple, who have been here several years. The other three are also rented, but the tenants seldom stay long. At the time of writing, one was occupied by a Greek and one by an Albanian; the third was empty.

Behind my apartment block, there is a larger complex of apartments, also originally used for short-term holiday lets. Most of them are now empty, but some are occupied by single Pakistani men. There is a small but significant number of Pakistani migrant workers in Aghios Nikolaos – sufficiently large to warrant a shop selling Pakistani food. My neighbours are employed as manual labourers, often on a casual basis. In their spare time they play cricket in what was once the swimming pool!

I bought my apartment from one of a number of local estate agents that specialise in the sale of property to expatriates. The business was owned by an Englishman married to a Croatian woman. I have had a considerable amount of work done on the apartment since I bought it. Most was done by a self-employed Englishman, who was recommended to me by my English neighbour. During the three years that I knew him, he employed various assistants on a casual basis, including an Albanian, a West African and an Algerian. My current 'odd job man' is a Greek married to an Englishwoman.

My apartment is about 25 minutes' walk from the centre of Aghios Nikolaos. However, there are two food shops quite near. The largest is Lidl, the German supermarket chain that has spread into many parts of Europe, including the UK. It has branches throughout Crete. I do most of my shopping there, primarily because of its proximity but also because for most things it is significantly cheaper than the local Greek supermarkets. The other is the British Food Shop, which is owned by a Greek man married to an Englishwoman. It serves the expatriate British community, not just in Aghios Nikolaos but in much of eastern Crete. Since I prefer to eat local Greek produce, I seldom buy food there. However, I patronise it regularly because it runs a free book exchange, specialising of course in English language books. It is my local library!

My nearest beach, Almyros, is about twenty minutes' walk away. As I mentioned in Chapter 2, it is a lovely beach and I go there at least once a day, but in summer I have to share it with a large number of tourists. They come from many different parts of the world, but the majority are Russians. There are three hotels near Almyros. They are all owned by Greeks, but one is managed by an Englishwoman. On my way to the beach, I pass some holiday apartments run by a German couple and when my foster daughter and her partner visited me in 2014 they stayed in a Russian-owned hotel in the town centre.

I have, as I will explain later, made various attempts to learn Greek since I came to Crete. I have attended many different classes and, in those classes, my fellow students have come from sixteen different countries: Belgium, France, Germany, Ireland, the Netherlands, Portugal, Switzerland and the UK in Western Europe; Belarus, Russia, Romania, Slovenia and Ukraine in Eastern Europe; and further afield, Australia, Uganda and even the Dominican Republic.

My situation is not unusual. Rackham and Moody suggest (in the quotation at the beginning of the chapter) that Crete has always been a cosmopolitan place, but that is truer than ever now. It is now not only an integral part of Greece but also a member of the European Union (EU) and part of an increasingly 'globalised' world. In the last three or four decades, the combined forces of Europeanisation and globalisation have resulted in another invasion: an invasion of people, products, capital, economic policies, and rules and regulations, from other EU countries and from other parts of the world.

This chapter describes this contemporary invasion. It examines four main manifestations of it: tourism; other forms of trade and investment; migration; and political domination. In each case, we will look at the form the invasion takes and its impact on the island. There are two main aims. One is to give an idea of what Crete is like today – both as a place to visit and as somewhere to live or work. The other is to explore Crete's increasingly complex relationship with the outside world. We will examine three 'lay-ers' of this relationship: that with the rest of Greece, that with the EU and that with the rest of the world. In the conclusion, I will attempt to compare this invasion with the earlier ones described in Chapter 3.

Tourism

> Crete is in many respects the culmination of the Greek experience. (*Lonely Planet* website)

Tourism is the most visible aspect of Crete's latest invasion. Over the last half century, it has been transformed from a quiet, little known island into one of the world's most popular tourist destinations. As the above quotation suggests, it is an ideal tourist location. It combines a Mediterranean climate with spectacular scenery, abundant relics of its fascinating historical past, and a vibrant culture. There is something for everyone in Crete.

Growth of the tourist industry

Tourism began in the 1960s and early 1970s, when, as I mentioned in Chapter 3, the island was a popular retreat for backpackers and hippies. Some friends from London, who visited me here in 2014, drew my attention to a song by Canadian folk singer, Jodi Mitchell, about the little south coast resort of Matala, where she stayed in the late 1960s. The song, which is called 'Carey', refers to 'the wind from Africa' and 'the scratchy rock-and-roll beneath the Matala moon'.[90]

Over the next two decades the industry grew slowly; but then in the 1990s, there was a sudden boom. The number of international arrivals increased from 1.5 million in 1990 to 2.5 million in 1997. The increase continued, albeit more slowly, until 2007, when the number of arrivals reached 2.8 million. There was then a four year period in which the industry stagnated, with numbers returning to the 1997 level. This was due to the repercussions of the 2008 financial crisis, which I will discuss later in the chapter.

However, in 2012 it began to pick up again and in 2014 the number of arrivals reached an all-time high of over 3.5 million.[91]

These figures are based on international arrivals by air, and thus exclude air travellers from other parts of Greece and those arriving by sea. Although these numbers are small in comparison to the international air travellers, they are not insignificant, particularly those arriving by sea. There is a daily ferry service from the mainland to both Iraklio and Chania and, during the summer, many cruise ships visit these two ports and some come to Aghios Nikolaos. In the summer of 2014, there were two cruise ships that visited Aghios Nikolaos every week. They spent a day in the town, arriving early in the morning and leaving in the evening.

Types of tourists

Crete attracts many different types of tourist. However, at the risk of some oversimplification, one can identify four main types: beach-lovers, sightseers, night-clubbers and explorers.

Nearly everyone who visits Crete spends some time on the beach. However, in Crete as in many other parts of the world, there is a particular type of tourist who spends virtually all the time on the beach. These are the beach-lovers. They tend to go to the same beach every day, usually the one nearest to the place where they are staying. They arrive mid-morning, acquire sunbeds and a sunshade, apply a liberal coat of sunscreen lotion, and stay until late-afternoon. My nearest beach, Almyros, is a good place to find the typical beach-loving tourist.

The sightseers are more ambitious than the beach-lovers. They come armed with their guidebooks, determined to see as much as possible. However, they tend to follow well established 'tourist trails' that incorporate the best-known and best-advertised sights. These include archaeological sites, places of historical and cultural interest, and areas of natural beauty. Aghios Nikolaos is a popular base for the sight-seeing tourist. The town itself is attractive, with its sandy coves, picturesque streets and the mysterious Lake Voulismeni. And there are many places within easy travelling distance, ranging from the archaeological sites at Gournia and Lato to the palm fringed beach at Vai and the little rocky island of Spinalonga, whose fascinating history makes it probably the most popular tourist attraction in the area.

The night-clubbers are a smaller group. Like the beach-lovers, they spend much of the time on the beach and seldom travel far afield. However, their main interest is the nightlife. The typical night-clubber is young, comes from the UK and travels to Crete with a group of friends, often of the same sex. They congregate in resorts that cater specifically for their interests: places where there are numerous bars and nightclubs that stay open all night, the cafes and restaurants serve American-style fast food as well as Greek dishes, and English is widely spoken. The most popular area is a chain of resorts along the north coast east of Iraklio, the largest being Malia and Hersonnissos. I feel sorry for the local people who live or work in this area. Drunkenness and drink-related violence are significant problems. In the early hours of the morning, drunken youths roam the streets and fights often break out.

I tend to avoid these areas. However, in November 2014 I met someone with an inside view. Ivor (not his real name) is a former long-distance lorry driver from the UK. He and his wife retired to Crete a few years before I met him. Since they retired early, they had to work for the first couple of years. So they both got summer jobs in the Malia branch of the fast-food chain Subway. His wife worked the day shift and Ivor the night shift. He loved the job and was fascinated by the people he met. Although many of his clients were too drunk to carry on a coherent conversation, he was able to talk to some of them. He was surprised to find that many were college graduates. Some had actually come to Crete to celebrate their recent graduation. He tried to tell them that there was much more to Crete than beaches and night clubs and encouraged them to go out and explore the island. Apparently a few took his advice and on their return came and told him how impressed they had been.

The explorers are another relatively small group and their presence is less obvious than the others. This is because they go off the beaten track. They may stay in one of the popular resorts, but they use this merely as a base, from which they explore the lesser known parts of the island. They may visit some of the many unpublicised Minoan sites, discover remote churches or monasteries, relax on secluded beaches, eat in small village tavernas or go for long walks in the hills. The more adventurous can even go rock climbing in the Cha Gorge. My friends from London, who drew my attention to Jodi Mitchell's song about Matala, are typical explorers. Bill and Liz (not their real names) spent ten days in Crete. They went to many of the well-known tourist sights, but did not stop there. Like most explorers, they are experienced travellers. They have lived and worked in many parts of the world and, at the time of their visit, one of their ongoing projects was to walk round the coast of England and Wales. They were doing it in stages, a few miles at a time.

Tourist origins

Where do these tourists come from? The simple answer is from all over the world. There are tourists from other parts of Greece, from other EU countries, and from other parts of the world. A brief look at each of these groups will give some idea of the nature of Crete's current tourist invasion.

The Greek tourists are difficult to identify. Since they are not foreign nationals their arrival is not recorded and since they speak the same language it is not easy to distinguish them from the local population. However, the general impression one gets, particularly from visits to local tourist attractions, is that there are a significant number, but less than from other countries. I suspect that the majority would fit into the sightseer category. In the Aghios Nikolaos area, the most likely place to see them is at

Spinalonga. I am told that they do not like to be lumped together with other tourists; they regard themselves as 'Greeks on holiday' rather than 'tourists'.

Residents of other EU countries constitute the largest group of tourists. The majority come from north-western Europe, especially the UK and Germany, but also France, the Netherlands and Scandinavia. These are the tourists who 'discovered' Crete and accounted for the boom in the 1990s. Initially, most of them came on 'package tours' - that is, holidays in which travel, accommodation and often also sight-seeing trips are booked as a package. This type of holiday is still popular (that was how my husband and I initially visited Crete), but many people now make their own travel and accommodation arrangements.

These tourists span all four of the groups described above (beach-lovers, sightseers, night-clubbers and explorers); however, as I have already indicated, the British have the dubious reputation of being the main night-clubbers. Similarly, although European tourists are found throughout the island, there is a tendency for some nationalities to concentrate in particular areas. This is due partly to airline schedules. For example, German and in particular Scandinavian airlines tend to fly to Chania rather than Iraklio, so there are more tourists from these countries in the western part of the island. However, there are also particular places that are popular with certain groups. An interesting example is the little village of Myrtos, which is located on the south coast a few kilometres west of Ierapetra. It is a popular tourist destination, particularly but not only among Germans, and it tends to attract a particular type of tourist, including those who in the 1960s or '70s would have been regarded as hippies. It has shops selling Indian as well as locally-made clothes and handicrafts, a *taverna* that plays folk music, and courses in yoga and meditation.

Although EU residents still constitute the majority of tourists, their dominant position is now being challenged by visitors from outside the EU. In recent years, Greece as a whole, and Crete in particular, has become very popular with tourists from Eastern Europe, especially Russia. By 2012, Russia ranked fourth in terms of the number of tourists visiting Greece, after Germany, the UK and France.[92] At the time of writing, there was concern that the number might fall, due to the deterioration in the Russian economy and, in particular, the exchange rate between the rouble and the euro. However, if it happens, this will probably be only a temporary decline. Greece's popularity with Russian tourists stems primarily from increasing incomes and changing life-styles in Russia, but also from the close links between the Russian and Greek orthodox churches.

Most of the Russian tourists are beach-lovers. They come on package holidays and stay in relatively large hotels where all meals are provided as part of the package. Some people criticise them for this. But in my view, it is understandable, given the history of tourism in Russia. In the Soviet era, the state owned hotels on the Black Sea where most workers spent their annual summer holiday. International tourism is a relatively new phenomenon and Russians are understandably wary of fending for themselves in a strange country where they do not understand the language or the customs. Western European tourists were the same in the 1950s and '60s; hence the birth of the package holiday. The Russians will no doubt become more adventurous over time.

The Russian tourists tend to concentrate in particular parts of the island. Aghios Nikolaos is one such area. This is reflected in the large number of Russian tourists on beaches like Almyros and the presence of several Russian-owned hotels in the area. It is also reflected in the fact that my various attempts to learn Greek, which I will describe in Chapter 6, included attending two summer courses for Russian students visiting the area. The courses are organised by the local Church for members of the Russian Orthodox Church who come to learn more about both the Greek language and the Greek Church.

There are also a number of tourists from other parts of the world, including the USA and Australia and, recently, an increasing number from East Asian countries, including South Korea, Japan and China. These tourists tend to belong to the sightseer category. The East Asians often visit Crete as part of some sort of European tour. In March 2015 a Chinese cruise ship with 800 passengers spent a day in Iraklio. They were on a 12-week trip, which would take them to 28 destinations in 18 different countries.[93] However, Crete is also becoming increasingly popular as a place where Chinese people come to get married – although not as popular as the neighbouring island of Santorini. They come in groups, so the weddings are massive events.

Investment in tourism

Crete's tourist industry is based on the concept of the package holiday and although many tourists now come independently, it is still basically a package holiday destination. This is reflected in the pattern of investment. Since the main feature of a package holiday is that all components of the trip are booked together in the country of origin, much of the investment in tourism is by companies from these countries. The best way to examine the pattern of investment is thus to look at the origins and evolution of the package holiday industry.

The concept of the package holiday was born in north-western Europe. The traditional package consisted of a charter flight to the destination, accommodation, transport to and from the airport, a representative on site, and (usually an optional extra) day trips to places of interest. Booking were made through a tour operator in the home country, such as Thomas Cook or Tui. The charter flights were operated by airlines also based in the country of origin, sometimes normal commercial operators but more often special charter airlines, often owned by the tour operators. A choice of accommodation, including hotels and self-catering facilities, was usually offered. In some parts of the world, these establishments were also owned by companies from the home country, but in Crete most were Greek-owned. They included some large hotels owned by companies based in mainland Greece, but also many smaller establishments run as family businesses by local Cretan people. The tour operators had an arrangement with selected establishments in each location, guaranteeing them a regular flow of guests in return for concessionary prices. Transport to and from the airport was provided either in coaches owned and run by the tour operators or through contracts with local companies, and the local representatives were from the home country and employed directly by the tour operators.

Although many tourists from north-western Europe still come on such packages, there have, in Crete as elsewhere, been some changes in their mode of operation. The main one has been the rise of budget airlines, which have partially but not totally replaced the traditional charter flights. The most obvious example, at least in Crete, is EasyJet, which operates scheduled flights to Crete from several UK airports throughout the summer season. Although the larger companies like Thomas Cook and Tui still operate their own flights, many tour operators now book their clients on EasyJet. Incidentally, the founder and main shareholder of Easyjet is a Greek businessman; however, the company is registered in the UK so Greece presumably gains little financial benefit other than landing fees.

We have also seen that an increasing number of tourists from this region travel independently. There are two main reasons for this. One is that tourists today are more experienced and adventurous than they were. The other is that it is cheaper and easier than it was to make one's own travel arrangements, due in part to the existence of budget airlines but also to online booking services. It is now very easy not only to book flights online but also, thanks to companies such as Booking.com and TripAdvisor (both of which incidentally are registered in the United States), to book accommodation. However, even in these arrangements, elements of the traditional package holiday remain. For example, the budget airlines have links with other service providers, so when you book a ticket online, they do their best to sell you other components of your holiday, such as accommodation, car hire and travel insurance. These complex linkages are typical of the global world in which we now live.

In Russia, however, the situation is rather different. Here the concept of a package holiday has been reborn and extended. As I mentioned earlier, most Russian tourists come on package tours and in many cases all components of these packages are Russian owned. The tourists do not only book through a Russian tour operator and travel on a Russian airline; many also stay in Russian-owned hotels. A Russian company called Dessole Resort and Hotels has recently bought six large hotels in Crete, including three of the largest in or near Aghios Nikolaos. The other three are in Ierapetra, Malia and a resort west of Iraklio. The company, which also has hotels in Egypt and Tunisia, is an offshoot of a large tour operator called Pegas Touristik, which also owns the airline that brings the tourists to Crete. The company thus provides a complete tourist package.

Impact of tourism

Tourism is one of the two main pillars of the Cretan economy, the other being agriculture. It is the main source of revenue and employment in the island.[94] Moreover, many other economic activities, particularly those in the retail and service sectors, are indirectly dependent on it. There is no doubt that, without tourism, Crete would be a much poorer place – and also a very different place.

One might argue that Crete does not receive as much income from tourism as it could or should because many of the tourists come on package holidays, where the profits accrue to the foreign-owned tour operator and airline. Moreover, some stay in all-inclusive, foreign-owned hotels. However, even in these cases there is some benefit to the local economy.

One can also argue that in Crete, as elsewhere, tourism has its costs. One such cost is the risk to the environment. In this respect, the situation in Crete is not as bad as that in many parts of the world, since the government has attempted to regulate tourist-related development and protect areas of natural significance - such as the reed-beds at Almyros beach. Moreover, it is in Crete's interest to protect its natural environment, because it is one of the features that attracts tourists to the island. However, there is inevitably some conflict of interest between investment in tourism and environmental protection. The government's attempt to allow private developers exclusive access to parts of the coast, which I mentioned in Chapter 2, is clear evidence of this. However, the fact that this attempt failed is encouraging.

Tourism also puts a strain on public services. Crete's native population is small. In 2011, when the last population census was taken, it was estimated to be only 574,000. An annual influx of nearly four million tourists thus makes a significant difference. If one assumes that 80% of arrivals occur during the main tourist season, which runs from May to October, and that the average stay is a week, the population of Crete increases by nearly 20% during these six months. Moreover, since most tourists tend to concentrate in the main towns and resorts, the impact in these areas is even greater. This inevitably presents a challenge for the local authorities.

An obvious example of this, and one that also has environmental implications, is solid waste removal. One needs only to visit a popular beach at the end of a hot summer day to get some idea of the scale of the problem. The number of plastic bottles discarded is of particular concern. Although the tap water in Crete is safe to drink, many people (including residents) prefer to buy bottled water - and in the height of summer one needs to consume large quantities of liquid. The costs of collecting and disposing of all this rubbish are high, especially on a small mountainous island like Crete where both landfill and recycling facilities are limited. Moreover, the local authorities have to comply with the EU's strict regulations regarding waste disposal. If there are any violations of these regulations, they have to pay a fine. These fines are levied on the Greek government, but in 2014 the government passed them on to local authorities.

Another example is airport services. There are two main international airports: Iraklio and Chania. The pressure on Iraklio is particularly high. In winter, the airport is very quiet. There are only a dozen or so flights a day and they are all domestic flights, mainly to Athens. But in summer it is a totally different place. There are hundreds of flights a day, most of them international. They arrive and depart at all hours of the day and night and are packed with tourists. There are plans to build a new airport some distance east of the city, but this will require time and money.

Tourism thus has costs as well as benefits. However, there seems little doubt, at least in the minds of most Cretans, that on balance it is beneficial. In a survey of nearly 200 urban residents published in 2004, 75% of respondents agreed with the statement that 'the benefits of tourism are greater than the costs to Crete as a whole', while only 11% disagreed.[95]

Other Trade and Investment

The first thing god made is the long voyage. (Giorgos Seferis, Greek poet, 1900-71)

As we saw in Chapter 3 and the above quotation suggests, Crete has always been a trading nation, with links to many parts of the Mediterranean and even further afield. Since it is now an integral part of Greece, it is difficult to get trade and investment statistics just for Crete. However, the information that is available suggests that this is still the case today. In fact, the twin processes of Europeanisation and globalisation have probably increased its relationships with other parts of the world. In this section, I will try to give some idea of the nature and scope of these relationships. Because of the lack of statistical data, I will draw mainly on my own observations and experiences. I will distinguish three main types of relationship: those with the rest of Greece, those with other EU countries, and those with other parts of the world.

Greece

Despite the lack of statistical data, it is evident simply from casual observation that Crete's main trading partner is, as one would expect, the rest of Greece. The nature of the relationship reflects the structure of Crete's economy, which, as we have seen, is based on agriculture and tourism. Thus, in the case of trade, Greece provides a market for much of Crete's agricultural produce and in return supplies a large proportion of its manufactured goods. In the case of investment, the relationship is more one-sided, the main investment being from the rest of Greece to Crete. The most obvious evidence of this is the presence in Crete of many large national companies, including banks, supermarket chains, media enterprises and the bus company KTEL. However, as we will see in the next chapter, these companies have not prevented Crete from retaining its own economic identity.

Other EU countries

According to Enterprise Greece, a government agency that promotes trade and investment, in 2013 nearly half of Greece's trade (46% of exports and 47% of imports) was with other EU countries. In the case of exports, the main EU partners were Italy, Germany and Bulgaria, followed by Cyprus, Gibraltar and the UK, and in the case of imports, Germany and Italy, followed by France and the Netherlands. It also informs us that in the decade from 2003 to 2013, most foreign investment in Greece was from the EU, with three countries, Germany, France and the UK, dominating the scene.[96] In order to give some idea of what these figures mean in practice, I will look briefly at the role of three of these countries: Germany, Italy and the UK, focusing on the visible evidence of their role in Crete.

Germany is the main investor in the country as a whole and over the last decade the volume of its investment has increased significantly, while that from France has remained much the same and that from the UK has declined. Of particular significance is the fact that German investment increased during the period when Greece faced severe economic problems and was forced to borrow large sums of money from the EU and the IMF. The implications of this will be discussed later.

German investment in Crete is most obvious in the retail sector. As I mentioned earlier, the cut price German supermarket chain, Lidl, has established itself in Crete. It has eleven stores on the island, including three in Iraklio and one in each of the other main towns. It is the only non-Greek supermarket company, but because its prices are significantly lower than those in the Greek stores, it poses a serious threat to them, especially at a time when money is scarce. In the four years that I have been shopping at my local Lidl store, I have noticed a significant increase in the number of customers, and particularly in the number of Greeks. On a Saturday morning, the store is packed.

Shopping in Lidl is an interesting experience. A few years before I moved to Crete, a branch of Lidl opened near my home in the UK and I often shopped there. The two stores are remarkably similar. The layout is almost the same, as is the range of household goods on special offer, which changes every week. However, there are also subtle but significant differences. Lidl is very good at adapting to meet local demand. For example, my local store sells a wide range of food that is popular in Greece, such as soft cheeses, yogurts, Greek-style coffee, rusks and seasonal specialities, and omits some of the things common in its UK shops, including most tinned goods and other sorts of processed food.

It also adjusts its suppliers, presumably with the aim of finding the cheapest sources. In Crete, I buy the same German beer and cakes that I bought in the UK and also a German brand of coffee. But most of my other regular purchases come from Greece, or in a few cases from neighbouring countries. For example, the bread comes from a local bakery up the road in Kritsa, the olive oil from Chania, dairy products from mainland Greece (the fresh milk comes all the way from Macedonia), and margarine from Slovakia. Lidl also sells fruit and vegetables, most of which come from Greece, but I prefer to buy these from a local greengrocer or the weekly market because they are fresher.

Lidl's marketing strategies are also good. They not only advertise widely, but also promote themselves as a 'socially responsible' company. For example, my local store, like several other supermarkets in the area, operates a 'food bank', where customers can donate food items (purchased in the store, of course) which are then distributed by a local voluntary organisation to needy people in the town.

Lidl is not the only German retail company competing in Crete. In Iraklio there are branches of two other major chains, Praktiker (a furniture and do-it-yourself store) and Makro (a cut-price wholesaler, originally Dutch but now owned by the German company Metro). Both provide serious competition for the local Greek companies, especially in terms of price. However, Praktiker also faces some competition from the Swedish company Ikea, which opened a store in Iraklio in 2013.

Other forms of German involvement are less visible but equally if not more significant, especially since some involve state-owned activities. They include investment in infrastructure and telecommunications and the sale of equipment to the Defence Forces. Deutsche Telekom, for example, is the largest shareholder in OTE, the main telecommunications company. Both Deutsche Telekom and OTE were originally state-owned companies, and their respective governments still hold some shares. And at the time of writing, there were plans, as part of the Greek government's privatisation programme, to contract out the operation of fourteen regional airports to a consortium involving a German company (the main shareholder of which is the German state) and a Greek firm. Included in the fourteen is Crete's second largest airport, at Chania. The remaining airports will be operated by a Greek company.[97]

The *United Kingdom*'s involvement, although less important than that of Germany in Greece as a whole, is very evident in Crete. One of the most obvious examples to me, probably because I am one of them, is the large number of British people with holiday or retirement homes on the island. From the late-1990s until 2008, the Cretan property market boomed, fuelled partly by the growth in tourism but also by the large number of foreigners wanting to buy property. The British were not the only investors, as the mix of nationalities in my own block of apartments testifies, but they constituted the majority. Crete was, of course, not the only place to attract such investment. During this period, many British people bought holiday or retirement homes elsewhere in Europe, including other parts of Greece, France and, in particular, Spain. But it was one of the most popular.

In Crete, as elsewhere, the overseas property market collapsed after the 2008 European financial crisis and, unlike tourism, has been slow to recover. Property prices plummeted and, due to the combination of lack of demand and property owners' reluctance to reduce prices, the market ground to a halt. In mid-2010, only six months after buying my apartment, I decided to try to sell it because, due to my husband's ill-health, I had no idea if or when I would be able to live there. It was on the market for two years and during that time no one even came to look at it. Meanwhile, the apartment above mine, which was for sale for 45,000 euros when I bought mine, remained empty until mid-2013, when it was bought by my English neighbour for 23,000 euros. However, many if not most of those who had already bought properties remained in Crete after the crash. I will say more about some of these people in the next section of the chapter.

Another example of British involvement, and one closely related to the large number of British expatriates, is the British Food Shop, which, as I mentioned earlier, is (purely by coincidence, I hasten to add) my nearest food shop. It is, as far as I know, the only such shop on the island. Having lived in a town in the UK with a shop specialising in South African food, I was interested but not surprised to find a similar phenomenon in Crete. There is also a transport company, called Nomad, which specialises in the movement of goods between the UK and Crete. The goods are transported most of the way overland in the company's own truck. If there is sufficient demand, it makes a return journey once a month. Nomad's head office is in the UK, but it has a base at Vamos in western Crete. I used it to bring out some of my personal possessions when I moved here.

British companies have also penetrated the general retail market in Crete, although to a lesser extent than those of Germany. The most obvious example is Marks and Spencer, which has a branch in Iraklio. More significant, however, is the role of the British telecommunications company Vodaphone, which has captured a large share of the Greek mobile phone market. It is one of the three main mobile phone companies in Greece. The other two, COSMOTE (which is part of OTE) and WIND, are Greek. Vodaphone's role is significant not just because it is an international company but also because mobile phones have revolutionised global communication. Like Lidl, Vodaphone promotes itself as a socially responsible company, sponsoring a wide range of social activities.

Italy's role in Crete is less visible than those of Germany and the UK. However, it is an important trading partner because much of Crete's olive oil is exported to Italy, where it is blended with some of Italy's poorer quality oils and then re-exported. I do not know what the main imports from Italy are, but I would guess that, as in many other European countries, they include 'white' goods - that is, things like fridges, freezers and washing machines. Both my fridge and my washing machine are Italian.

Other parts of the world

Although the EU remains the main trading and investment partner, relationships with other countries are, as in the case of tourism, becoming increasingly important. The two main new players are Russia and China. Their role is expanding rapidly and
their presence becoming increasingly obvious.

The importance of trade between Greece and Russia became
evident in 2014, when the crisis in Ukraine sparked a conflict between the EU and Russia. The EU imposed sanctions on Russia
because of its role in Ukraine and Russia reacted by placing an
embargo on many exports from EU countries. It emerged that
Greece was exporting large quantities of fruit and vegetables to
Russia, including half its peach crop. Since the embargo was imposed at the height of the peach season, it caused chaos. Trucks
of rotting fruit were stuck at border posts and had to be thrown
away. Greek farmers were furious and demanded compensa-
tion from the EU. I don't know what proportion of these exports
come from Crete. However, although relatively far from Russia,
it is one of Greece's main fruit and vegetable growing regions
and it was evident from the concern expressed in the local media
that many Cretan farmers were affected.

The crisis in Ukraine also raised concerns about the future of
the country's energy supplies, since, following the imposition of
sanctions against Iran, Russia had become Greece's main source
of oil and natural gas. Thus, as in many other European countries, the crisis sparked debates about alternative sources, including the possibility of exploiting the substantial reserves of natural gas believed to exist off the southern coast of Crete.

Although oil and gas are the main imports from Russia, they are
not the only ones. One of the more unexpected is Russian television programmes. The Greek television stations rely heavily
on imported films and soap operas, which are rebroadcast with
Greek sub-titles. Most of these originate from America and to a

lesser extent the UK and France. But there are a significant number from Russia.

The most obvious sign of *China*'s involvement is the large number of 'China shops'; that is, shops selling Chinese products. When I first came to Aghios Nikolaos there were seven such shops, but one has since closed. Four of the six are in the same street. They all sell the same range of goods for the same prices. Clothing predominates, but a variety of other products (such as blankets, suitcases, cheap radios and toys) are also sold. Since the prices, especially of the clothes, are low compared with those in other shops, they attract a considerable number of local residents, especially those in lower income groups and people (like me) who are always on the lookout for a bargain. However, although the number of customers has increased in recent years, there are seldom more than two or three in a shop at any one time and they are often just browsing. This is not surprising, since it seems unlikely that Aghios Nikolaos, which has a population (even if one includes the hinterland) of only about 27,000, can support six such shops. I often wonder how and why they keep going.

Chinese shops are a common phenomenon throughout Greece. Apparently, they penetrated the market at a time of economic boom and, then, when the economy collapsed, capitalised on the increasing demand for cheap goods.[98] In the big cities, especially Athens, there is a significant Chinese population and, as in so many parts of the world, many Chinese restaurants. In Crete, however, there are very few Chinese restaurants. There is only one in Aghios Nikolaos.

Less obvious but probably of more economic significance, is China's increasing involvement in other sectors of the Greek economy, especially infrastructure. China appears to see the privatisation of Greek infrastructure as a means of increasing its involvement in the country – and in Europe. For example, the China Ocean Shipping Company (COSCO) has a major stake in the port of Piraeus, while another company owns several shipyards.

Chinese companies are also apparently interested in a number of other infrastructure projects, including the construction of a new airport in Crete, which will eventually replace the overstretched one at Iraklio.[99]

Impact of trade and investment

The effects of this trade and investment are difficult to calculate and probably more mixed than those of tourism. On the one hand, there have undoubtedly been benefits, particularly for consumers. These include cheaper goods, more choice and competition in service provision, and improved infrastructure. For example, in the retail sector, the relatively cheap price of basic food items in Lidl and clothes in the Chinese shops has helped people make ends meet during the recent period of recession and austerity. Similarly, in the case of telecommunications, people say that the former state-owned company, OTE, is now much more efficient than it was, while Vodaphone has increased the competition among mobile phone providers. And in the case of infrastructure, there is no doubt that Iraklio needs a new airport and this is unlikely to occur without external investment, whether from China or elsewhere.

Crete has also benefited from the expansion of international trade by exporting its own produce, particularly olive oil, fruit and vegetables. And the property boom was beneficial while it lasted. Prices soared, thus not only creating income for those who chose to sell but also stimulating much new construction and thus generating employment.

However, there have also been costs, particularly for local enterprises, such as shops. For example, the increase in the number of people shopping at Lidl and in the Chinese shops in recent years must have had a negative impact on local stores, while the purchase of several large hotels by Russian companies must have had a similar effect on the local hotel trade. In the case of Chinese investment, there is an additional problem, in that the working conditions are often poor and Chinese workers are imported to do jobs that could be done by locals. There has been much criticism of the Chinese shipping company, COSCO, in this respect. And there was also a downside to the property boom, in that it became more difficult for local people to buy property.

Another, rather different issue is that of corruption. There have been three prominent cases of investment-related corruption in recent years, all involving German companies. The first concerned a contract awarded in 1998 to the German company Siemens for the digitalisation of the telephone company, OTE, which at that time was still owned by the state. It apparently involved around 70 million euros in bribes. The other two related to the sale of defence equipment to the state, one by Daimler and the other by a company called Krauss-Maffei Wegmann. The first was reputed to have involved bribes of about two million euros and the second 1.5 million.[100] These incidents contributed to the emergence of an increasingly negative feeling about Germany during the period of economic decline and austerity. Germany was not only benefitting from Greece's misfortunes by lending it money and taking over its economy, but also ripping it off and fuelling one of its greatest problems – corruption.

Migration

The grass is always greener on the other side. (English proverb)

The search for greener pastures has in the past brought many migrants to Crete and it continues to do so today. The movement is not only one-way. In times of hardship, such as the recession that followed the 2008 financial crisis, many Cretans leave the island, in search of work on the mainland or further afield. The man who looks after the apartment next to mine illustrates this point. He has two daughters in their early twenties who live and work in Thessaloniki and his brother, the owner of the apartment, works in Belgium. Many young Cretans also go to the mainland for tertiary education. Moreover, there is also migration within Crete. The main trend has been from rural areas to the towns, but the recent recession forced some people to move back to the villages where life is cheaper.

However, our interest here is in those migrants who are moving into Crete. At the risk of some over-simplification, these may be divided into four main types, based on a combination of their region of origin and their reasons for coming to the island: those from other parts of Greece, who come for a variety of reasons; those from countries more affluent than Greece who come primarily to work; those from more affluent countries who come not to work but to retire; and those from less affluent parts of the world, who come primarily to work. I have distinguished between more and less affluent countries rather than EU members and others because the affluence of the country of origin tends to determine the reasons for migrating and, in the case of 'economic' migrants, the types of jobs held.

I will look briefly at each of these types, using examples from people whom I have met. In order to protect these individuals, I will not in most cases use their real names. I will refer to them by a fictional first name. I will only use the real name when referring to someone who is publically known in some capacity or other (for example, has published work on Crete) and in these cases I will give both their first name and their surname.

Migrants from other parts of Greece

Since Crete is an integral part of Greece, there is inevitably much movement of people between the island and other parts of the country. Most Greeks who come to Crete are economic migrants; in other words, they come to work. They may be civil servants or employees of national companies who are posted to Crete, or job-seekers who come on their own initiative, attracted by employment opportunities in the tourist industry. A few years ago the apartment above mine was rented by a young woman from the mainland who had a summer job in a local hotel. However, work is not the only reason; for example, some come because their spouse is from Crete and, although the trend among students is mainly in the other direction, some come to study. I have a Greek friend who currently lives in the UK but came to Crete in 2014 to visit her niece and nephew, who were from the mainland but studying here. When I asked her why they had chosen Crete, she said that, as is so often the case with young people, they wanted to get away from home and see something of the world.

For an outsider like myself, it is difficult to distinguish between migrants from other parts of Greece and those born in Crete. I have to ask people where they come from. Moreover, there is much inter-marriage between the two groups and, since this movement of people has been going on since Greek colonisation began in the first century BC, there are probably very few people who can claim to be genuinely 'Cretan'. Nevertheless, we shall see in the next chapter that there is still a sense of Cretan identity among those born and brought up in the island.

Economic migrants from more affluent countries

Over the last three or four decades many people from countries more affluent than Greece have come to Crete to work. They have been attracted partly by the employment opportunities offered, especially those in the tourism and property industries, but also by the living and working conditions. Most come from EU member states but there are also some from further afield.

These migrants are generally employed in jobs that are relatively well-paid and/or require some sort of professional skills and many are self-employed. They stay for varying lengths of time, depending on their personal circumstances and the economic climate. Since the 2008 financial crisis, it has been more difficult both to find employment and to start one's own business and this has forced some people to leave. However, many others have stayed, often because they enjoy the life in Crete and in some cases because they have married local people and so regard Crete as their home. A few examples will give some idea of the range of people in this group.

The first one I met was Sandra, an English woman who was my main point of contact in the estate agency through which I bought my apartment. I had actually met her on an earlier visit to Aghios Nikolaos and her positive view of life in Crete was one of the factors that made my husband and I decide to move here. Her husband, Denis, worked in the same company, on the property development side. The company was, as I have already mentioned, owned by an English man married to a Croatian woman. It appears that this couple's main interest in Crete was to make money. When the property market collapsed, their company went bankrupt and they fled the country, leaving large debts and many dissatisfied clients. It was reputedly not the first country in which they had done this. Sandra and Denis were caught totally unaware. They went to work one morning to find the office locked and themselves unemployed. Since they were both nearing retirement age, they decided to stay in Crete and live off their pensions, but it was not an easy transition.

The next person I got to know well was Mark, the English builder who did the renovations on my apartment. Mark and his wife came to Crete by luck rather than by design. They were fed up with life in the UK and were thinking of moving to Malta. Then someone offered Mark a temporary building job in Crete. They had never been there, but they sold their house, packed up all their belongings and came. They ended up staying nearly ten years, during which time Mark built up a successful business. Their departure was almost as unexpected as their arrival; they went back to the UK for a three month visit and then decided to stay there, primarily for health reasons.

Some expatriates have unusual jobs. For example, Mandy does dog grooming and organises weddings. The main clients of her wedding business are tourists. It is not just the Chinese who come to Crete to get married. In many countries, including the UK, it is now fashionable to have an overseas wedding and Crete is becoming a popular location. Her husband, Larry is a self-employed motor mechanic and odd-job man. They live in Kritsa and have three teenage daughters. Mandy is English, but Larry is from South Africa. He is one of a number of South Africans living and working in the area. Others include Libby and Paul, who own a furniture store, and Sally, who works in a curio shop and does dressmaking.

Another expatriate with an interesting job is Gavin McGuire, a New Zealand-born archaeologist and photographer. He works on an archaeological site near Sissi, a village about 30 kilometres from Aghios Nikolaos, and has recently published a book about the site.[101] He is attached to the Belgian School in Athens, one of apparently 17 foreign archaeological institutes in Greece. The presence of these institutions reflects another dimension of the current invasion, one that (as we saw in Chapter 3) began in Crete with the arrival of archaeologists like Evans at the beginning of the 20th century.

There are also several teachers, including Derek from the UK who teaches English, Francesca from Italy who teaches Italian, and Annemarie, who is French and teaches Esperanto. Then there is an English couple who run a scuba-diving business, a Slovenian tour guide, and several artists of various nationalities. Two of these, Francesca and an American artist called Kathy, have lived in Crete for more than 20 years.

I mentioned earlier that some of these migrants marry Greeks and settle down in Crete. Becky and Andrea are two whom I know well. Both are English, have been in Crete for many years and have children in their twenties. They both came originally on working holidays soon after leaving school. Becky went back to the UK for a while to study, but then returned and got married. She and her husband own a shop in the town centre. They have two sons, one of whom is currently working in Crete and the other studying in the UK. Becky usually goes back to the UK at least once a year, mainly to visit her elderly parents. In Crete, she has a wide circle of friends, including both Greeks and expatriates.

Andrea's husband was a self-employed builder but is now retired. She has had various jobs, including one with an estate agency specialising in the sale of property to expatriates. They live on a smallholding a few kilometres outside Aghios Nikolaos. They have one daughter, who went to the UK to study a few years ago and is now working there. Andrea seems to have severed her links with the UK more than Becky. Although her daughter is there, she seldom goes back and she seems to have fewer expatriate friends than Becky.

It is not only English women who marry Greeks. Sabine Beckmann, the German archaeologist studying Minoan rural settlement in the Kroustas Forest, whom I mentioned in Chapter 3, is married to a Greek. So is the Italian teacher, Francesca. Other examples are Magda, Jean and Irma. Magda is Dutch. Her husband is a builder and she has a part-time job in a travel agency. Jean is Canadian. She and her husband have various business interests, including a fishmonger's shop. Irma is Russian. She and her husband work in the hotel trade. However, I only know one case of an expatriate man married to a Greek woman. He is Portuguese and teaches yoga and his wife is a psychotherapist. They met in the UK, where they were both studying. I am sure there are other cases, but they are certainly less common.

Retirees from more affluent countries

There is some overlap between economic migrants and retirees. For example, some people (like Sandra and Denis) come originally to work but after a few years retire. Others (like Ivor and his wife, who worked in Subway in Malia) come to retire, but do some casual work. And in some cases, one or more members of the family work, while others are retired. There is also some overlap between retirees and tourists. For example, there are many retired people who spend part of the year in Crete and part in their home country. My English, French and Serbian neighbours belong in this category. In this section, however, I will focus on those people who do little or no paid work and spend all or most of their time in Crete.

The retirees, thus defined, have two things in common: they are in the upper age brackets and they have some sort of independent income. In other respects, however, they vary greatly. They vary in their country of origin, their reasons for choosing Crete as a place to retire, their marital status and income, the type of home in which they live (bought or rented, large or small, rural or urban), and the way in which they spend their time. A few examples will illustrate this.

I am one of a relatively small number of single women. Some of these women were married when they came to Crete but, like me, are now widowed. One such person is Margaret. My husband and I met Margaret and her husband Bruce on one of our holidays to Crete. We were staying in the coastal village of Elounda and Margaret and Bruce lived in a rented apartment on the other side of the road. Their enthusiasm for life in Crete was one of the main factors that influenced our decision to come and live here. Margaret and I lost our husbands within a few months of each other. The difference was that Bruce died while living in Crete, while Ashley died before he could move here. I was surprised that Margaret decided to stay after Bruce died. I thought she would go back to the UK. I admired her decision and it encouraged me to come to Crete on my own.

Single men are also relatively rare. An interesting example is Alex, who has a relatively large apartment in an old building near the centre of Aghios Nikolaos. Alex was born in Cyprus but brought up in the UK. He decided long ago to retire overseas and after considering many other places (including his native Cyprus) chose Crete. He is more integrated into local society than most retirees, primarily because he speaks Greek well. Despite his Greek heritage, he did not learn the language as a child, so he has had to work hard to obtain such a high level of fluency. He is also very interested in Greek history, music and art.

Although many retirees choose to live on the coast, others prefer to live inland. One of the most popular inland locations is the Neapoli area. Neapoli itself is an old town that was once the administrative capital of the region. It is an interesting place, with a maze of narrow, winding streets and picturesque squares - and lots of unoccupied old houses ripe for modernisation. Ashley and I looked at one such property and for a few hours seriously considered buying it. However, we eventually decided against it, partly because we needed a place we could move into straight away but also because I wanted to be near the sea. There are also many attractive villages near Neapoli, some on relatively level ground in the Limnes valley and others in the hills surrounding the town.

Joan and Matthew live in a village in the Limnes valley. They bought some land and had a house built. They are English and aged in their seventies. For Joan and Matthew, it was a toss-up between Crete and Scotland! Joan wanted to go to Scotland and Matthew to Crete. Matthew's interest in Crete goes back a long way. He spent many holidays on the island and his daughter married a man from Kroustas, a village in the mountains inland from Aghios Nikolaos. His daughter subsequently died and her husband remarried, but he and Joan often got to Kroustas to visit his son-in-law's new family.

Although Joan and Matthew both have health problems, they are very active in the local expatriate community. Joan was for many years the treasurer of an organisation called the International Cultural Organisation of Aghios Nikolaos (of which I will say more in a later chapter) and Matthew helps to organise a photography club. Joan is also a very good dancer. One winter we went to Greek dancing classes together; I was hopeless and gave up after a few weeks, but she was excellent.

It is not unusual to find two generations of a family living in Crete, usually a married couple and one of more of their parents. Often the younger couple are still employed, but that is not always the case. For example, Judy and Ron live in a village in the hills east of Neapoli. Ron took early retirement, so they were relatively young when they moved to Crete. Soon after they arrived, Judy's parents, Elsie and Jim, came for a visit and decided to join them. After considering various options, they bought a house in the next village. Judy and Ron keep chickens and a large number of pets, and Judy, a qualified dog trainer, is kept busy advising people who have problems with their pets. Elsie and Jim are both very active and participate in a variety of social activities, in the village and in the wider expatriate community.

These are merely a small sample of the retirees living in or near Aghios Nikolaos. There are many others I could describe. For example, there is Francine, a fellow student in many of my Greek classes, who is Swiss and lives with her husband in Neapoli, and Hans, who was a professional musician in a well-known German orchestra before retiring to Kritsa. And then there are the 'boat people', like Rachel and Adrian, an English couple who sailed the Mediterranean for many years before selling their boat and building a house in Crete, and Tony Cross, the amateur geologist from whom I learned the truth about Lake Voulismeni, who lives on a yacht in the local marina. However, this is enough to give some idea of the range of people and lifestyles.

Migrants from less affluent countries

Most of the migrants in this group are economic migrants. However, they differ from the economic migrants discussed earlier in two ways. First, they come not just because of the attractions of Crete but also because of the lack of employment opportunities in their own countries. In other words, they are driven by both 'push' and 'pull' factors. Second, they are generally engaged in less skilled, lower income occupations.

There are migrants in both rural and urban areas. In the rural areas they are employed on big farms, such as those around Ierapetra, where large quantities of vegetables are grown in plastic greenhouses. The majority of these migrants are from the Balkan region, particularly Albania but also Romania and Bulgaria. There is a long history of migration from this region. Romanians and Bulgarians are now EU citizens and since 2009 have had the legal right to work in Greece. However, this has merely legalised a process that has been going on for years. In the towns, there is a wider variety of jobs. Many people work in the tourism and construction industries, often on a casual or seasonal basis. Some of these urban-based migrants are also from the Balkans, but others are from Asia, particularly Pakistan, and there are even a few from Africa.

My young Romanian neighbours are an example of the Balkan migrants. He works in the construction industry and she has a summer job in a laundry. They came to Crete eight years ago because of the lack of employment in their own country. And in an apartment block nearby, there is an Albanian couple. He does various casual jobs and she is a housewife. When I first arrived, there was also a Bulgarian woman in this block whom I got to know quite well. She was not formally employed, but had come to look after her elderly grandparents, who had been in Crete for many years. I felt sorry for her; her grandmother was bedridden so the work was not easy and she had left a husband and children back in Bulgaria.

Soon after I arrived in Crete I also met Ibrahim, who claimed to be the only African in Aghios Nikolaos. Ibrahim was from West Africa and he worked for my builder, Mark. He was somewhat reticent to tell his story. However, as far as I could gather, he came from a relatively well-off family but had been sent to Europe to make some big money. I think he spent time on the Greek mainland before coming to Crete and I assume that he entered the country unofficially. Like most Africans, he was proficient in languages. He spoke English, French, Arabic and Greek, as well as several African languages. His Greek was not very good, but enough to get by and far better than Mark's, so one of his jobs was to act as Mark's interpreter. In the summer of 2013, two friends from England visited me. One of them, Joseph, was originally from Ghana, so I introduced him to Ibrahim. The four of us went for a meal at a restaurant that Ibrahim recommended.

A few months later, Mark left Crete and Ibrahim was without work. I saw him a couple of times, but then he disappeared. It was nearly a year before I heard any news of him. I was eating in the same restaurant with some other friends, so I asked the owner, who appeared to have known him quite well, if he knew where he was. He said that he did not know for sure but had heard that he had been arrested. I was shocked but not surprised to hear this, since the government had been tightening up on illegal immigrants. I only hoped that he had been deported, rather than held indefinitely in one of the country's detention camps, which are reputed to be very unpleasant.

Ibrahim was one of many migrants who become 'trapped' in Crete, and in Greece as a whole. They came at a time when the economy was booming and jobs were plentiful. But after the 2008 financial crisis, the situation changed dramatically. Tourism declined, the property market collapsed and activity in the construction sector fell by 80%.[102] Unemployment thus soared, among both Greeks and migrants. Since then, most urban migrants have had to survive on casual work, often on a day-labour basis. Early every morning, one sees groups of men, mainly Pakistanis, standing at pick-up points on the edge of Aghios Nikolaos, hoping that this will be their lucky day. And an hour or so later, one will see many of them trudging back to the places where they stay - such as the apartment blocks near mine.

Some of these trapped migrants join the informal sector. In the summer, they can be seen selling goods on the streets or the beaches. When my Ghanaian friend, Joseph, visited, we spent an afternoon on the beach at Malia. It was not a particularly pleasant experience, since the beach was so crowded that one could hardly move. However, it was interesting because there were several African men and women walking up and down the beach, hawking a variety of items, mainly things like watches and trinkets but in some cases food. And because African tourists are a relatively rare phenomenon, they all stopped for a chat with Joseph. Most were from West Africa, particularly Nigeria. Like Ibrahim, they had come in search of good jobs, but now they were barely scraping a living from hawking.

Others seek help from the International Office of Migration (IOM), which provides financial and other assistance to those wishing to return to their home country. The IOM has recognised the problem in Greece, and there are posters in strategic places, such as bus stations and information centres, explaining what help they can provide and how to contact them. However, many migrants are reluctant to avail themselves of these services, especially if, as is the case with most of those from countries outside the EU, they are in the country illegally.

At this point, brief mention should be made of the role of refugees. The distinction between economic migrants and refugees is not always clear-cut. The term 'refugee' is usually used to refer to people who flee from their countries for fear of persecution and seek asylum in the recipient country. However, many people leave for a combination of political and economic reasons and some economic migrants try to claim asylum on political grounds.

Refugees have become a major problem in Greece. The majority come by boat. They are victims of the increasingly heavy traffic in human beings in the Mediterranean. Most are heading for northern European countries, such as the UK, Germany or Scandinavia. However, they enter Europe via countries like Italy, Malta and Greece, which act as 'gateways' to the rest of the continent. There are two main routes. One is from North Africa to Italy or Malta. It is the longest established of the two and used mainly by economic migrants from West Africa. The other is from Turkey to either Greece or Italy. This route is used by both refugees and economic migrants from Asia and by increasingly large numbers of refugees from the eastern Mediterranean, especially Syria. Both routes are fraught with danger, because the boats are over-crowded and often not seaworthy. Nearly 3,500 people lost their lives trying to cross the Mediterranean in 2014 and another 1,800 in the first four months of 2015, including about 900 in a single incident in April.[103]

It is the increased traffic on the second route that has caused the recent problems in Greece. In the first four months of 2015, 18,000 migrants reportedly arrived in the country by sea.[104] Crete has been less affected than many other parts of the country, because most boats head for the mainland or the more northerly islands. However, some end up in Crete, usually because their boat capsizes or breaks down in waters near the island. There was one such case in November 2014, when a vessel carrying 600 refugees from Turkey to Italy suffered engine failure in stormy seas south-east of Crete. The Greek coastguard service rescued the boat and towed it to the southern port of Ierapetra. The town was totally unprepared for such an onslaught, but with the help of the Red Cross, accommodation was organised in a basketball stadium. The refugees, who were mainly Syrians but included some Palestinians, Afghans and Iraqis, spent nearly two weeks in Ierapetra, before being moved to the mainland or, in a few cases, repatriated. They were very appreciative of the way in which they were treated in the town. Before they left, they staged an event to thank their hosts.

Impact of migration

Migration from more affluent countries has probably benefitted

Crete. It has brought skilled labour and foreign currency and in many cases generated income and employment. Moreover, economic migrants from these countries are relatively mobile; if employment opportunities decrease, as they did after the 2008 crisis, they move elsewhere. However, migration from less affluent countries is a more mixed blessing. When the economy was booming, there was a demand for unskilled labour and migrants from places like the Balkans and Pakistan helped to fill this gap. As elsewhere in Europe, these migrants were prepared to do jobs that local people shunned - and to do so for lower wages.

However, after 2008, these migrants became a problem rather than an asset, competing with local people for low-paid jobs. During the 2014-15 olive harvest, one of my Greek neighbours, whose once flourishing engineering business collapsed during the recession, was glad to get casual work picking olives. I would see him standing on the side of the road in the mornings, alongside my Pakistani neighbours, waiting for the vehicles that would take them to the picking areas. This problem has contributed to the rise, particularly on the Greek mainland but to some extent also on Crete, of an ultra-right party, Golden Dawn. And the increase in refugees from Syria and elsewhere has exacerbated the problem.

Political Domination

> The crisis has caused democracy to regress and this is perhaps the most dramatic side effect of our economic adventure. (Karolos Papoulias, then President of Greece, 24 July 2014)

We saw in Chapter 3 that for a large part of its history, Crete has been subject to the rule of some external power, and one could argue that this is the case today, since the island has very little autonomy in terms of formal governance. There are three interrelated reasons for this: firstly, Crete is an integral part of Greece; secondly, Greece is a member of the European Union and also of the Eurozone; and thirdly, we are living in a world where international politics and governance play an increasingly important role. This section explores the nature and impact of each of these three factors.

Greece

Crete does not have any special status within Greece. It is subject to the same laws, policies and administrative procedures as the rest of the country. It is one of seven administrative regions and has its own regional government. However, neither the regional government nor the lower level prefectural and municipal governments have significant powers. There have been many local government reforms over the last century, but the general direction of these reforms has been one of centralisation rather than decentralisation.[105]

As an integral part of Greece, Crete has had to endure many ups-and-downs in terms of the quality of governance, including, as we saw in Chapter 3, participation in two world wars and long periods of civil war and dictatorship. Since 1974, the situation has been more stable, but only relatively so. Greece's democratic government has been plagued by patronage and corruption, there have been many economic problems, and in the last few years the country has twice been on the point of being forced out of the Eurozone. I will say more about the last issue in the next section, when we look at Greece's relationship with the EU.

However, despite these problems, there has been little or no serious talk, among either politicians or the general public, about the possibility of becoming politically independent. In December 2013, a few months after I moved to Crete, the island commemorated the 100th anniversary of its union with Greece. I thought this might trigger some discussion about the desirability of the union, especially since it occurred at a time when the country was experiencing serious economic and political problems. But it did not appear to do so. It seemed to be a time for looking back at the island's past history, rather than looking forward, and for celebration rather than remorse.

Why is this? The main reason is probably the strong social, economic and political ties with the mainland, which is what led to the decision to join Greece in 1913. As we saw in Chapter 3, there has been movement of people between Crete and the mainland for thousands of years and the common language, religion and culture is a powerful bond. The island's involvement in modern Greek politics also goes back many years, to its participation in the struggle for Greek independence. We saw in Chapter 3 how the renowned Cretan-born politician, Eleftherios Venizelos, who played a major role in this struggle and went on to become prime minister of Greece, was instrumental in bringing about Crete's union with Greece. Today, Cretan politics are inextricably linked with those of the country as a whole; all the major national parties are represented on the island and there is no separate Cretan party.

However, there are other possible reasons. One is Crete's size. Although it is the largest island in Greece and its population exceeds that of Malta, many people would argue that it is too small to sustain an independent government. Another is the political fragmentation within the island. Cretan unity has always been hampered by internal conflicts and the local administrative structure exacerbates these. The administrative region of Crete was not created until 2011, as part of a major restructuring of local government. Prior to this restructuring, the island was divided into four prefectures (now officially known as regional units), which had been the main units of administration for centuries. Although most of their powers and functions were in 2011 transferred either to the regional government or to the lower level municipal governments, the prefectures continue to have a strong sense of social and political identity. Moreover, the prefecture boundaries are also the boundaries of parliamentary constituencies.

Another possible explanation, and one that is central to my argument, is that, although there have been problems, Crete has done relatively well out of the union, particularly in economic terms. It is difficult to assess the economic impact, partly because of the limited amount of regional data but also because there is no way of knowing what would have happened if the island had been independent. However, Crete's economy has undoubtedly grown since its unification with Greece and it is now one of the most affluent parts of the country. According to an EU survey, in 2013 Crete's gross domestic product (GDP) per capita was the fourth highest of the thirteen economic regions into which the country was divided for purposes of the survey.[106]

European Union

For most of its recent democratic history, Greece has been an integral part of Europe. It joined the EU (or the European Common Market, as it was then) in 1980, only six years after the restoration of democracy, and the Eurozone when it was established in 2001. It has therefore been subject to the various economic, social and, after the introduction of the euro, financial policies and controls imposed by Brussels, which have increased significantly over the years.

For many years the benefits to Greece of its membership of the EU outweighed any possible costs. It benefited not only in terms of trade, but also because, as one of the EU's poorer members, it received substantial amounts of financial support, including agricultural subsidies through the Common Agricultural Policy (CAP), and funding for a variety of projects, especially infrastructure.

Crete received its share of these benefits. Its farmers received subsidies for, among other things, the large numbers of olive trees and livestock. And it received funding for many development projects, including a new highway that will eventually run the whole length of the island, green energy projects that make use of its abundant supply of both sunshine and wind, and the restoration of many historical sites. An eight kilometre section of the new highway passes very near where I live, so I have witnessed its construction. It has taken years to complete and, since it includes a tunnel, an underpass and many cuttings through rocky hills, it must have cost a great deal. One could question the long-term benefits of this funding, since most of it has been in the form of loans which will eventually have to be repaid. But the responsibility for repayment will rest with the Greek government, not with Crete.

However, in 2008 the situation changed dramatically. I have already made several references to the 2008 financial crisis and the time has now come to examine it in more depth. The crisis, which began with the property crash in the US and the UK, spread quickly and plunged the whole of the western world into recession. The Eurozone was particularly badly affected and, within the Eurozone, Greece was most seriously hit. The country fell into a deep recession, including as we have seen a major decline in tourism and the collapse of the property market, and the Greek government was forced to admit to an enormous budget deficit. This deficit had actually been accumulating for many years, but had been ignored while the economy was doing well.

In 2009 the government was forced to seek financial assistance. After some deliberation, the EU agreed to provide such assistance, in conjunction with the International Monetary Fund (IMF). Greece received a series of 'bail-out' loans, stretching over a four-year period (2010-14) and amounting in total to about 240 million euros.[107] This was not free money. Not only would the loans have to be repaid, but they were subject to stringent conditions. The government was forced to implement severe 'austerity' measures, including reductions in statutory wage levels and state pensions, new forms of taxation, cuts in social and welfare expenditure, privatisation of many state services and assets, drastic cuts in the size of the public service and a complete overhaul of its mode of operation. The implementation of these reforms was overseen by the 'Troika', the collective name used in Greece to refer to the European Commission, the European Central Bank and the IMF.

Greece was not the only European nation that had problems at this time. Most countries, including the UK, experienced a period of recession and had to make major budgetary cuts and some, such as Spain, Portugal, Ireland and Cyprus, were also forced to seek financial assistance. Moreover, many of the structural reforms imposed upon Greece, such as cuts in public services and privatisation, had been introduced in the UK and many other western countries many years earlier, as part of the neoliberal reforms that began in the 1980s. However, nowhere in Europe was the recession as great or the reforms as drastic as in Greece.

For me, the situation was reminiscent of that in many African countries during the 1980s and 1990s. Due to the combination of a deteriorating external trade position and internal economic and political mismanagement, many such countries were forced to seek financial assistance from the World Bank and the IMF. And, as in Greece, this assistance came in the form of loans which would ultimately have to be repaid, albeit at relatively low rates of interest, and were subject to the same sort of conditions, including drastic cuts in government spending and a complete overhaul of the public sector. It is now widely recognised by students of development studies that these 'structural adjustment' programmes, as they were called, did not work. They failed to generate growth and caused a great deal of hardship, especially for the poor.[108]

It was the same story in Greece. The combined impact of the recession and the reforms was catastrophic. The country experienced six years of negative economic growth (2009-2014), during which time economic production declined by nearly 25% and household consumption by 26%.[109] Poverty increased to an unprecedented level (35% by the end of 2013), due to a combination of declining salary levels, increasing unemployment, higher taxation and cuts in public expenditure. Between 2008 and 2013, salaries fell by 35% and unemployment increased by 300%. In 2013 the general unemployment rate was 30% and that of young people over 50%. Between 2009 and 2011, total public expenditure declined by 30 million euros (10% of GDP); expenditure on health care decreased by 11% and that on social welfare by 12%.[110]

Crete did not suffer as badly as many parts of the country. For example, the decline in tourist numbers between 2009 and 2012, due to the economic and political crisis, was not as great in Crete as in some other parts of the country. Moreover, the effects, both of the fall in tourism revenue and of the various austerity measures imposed by the government during this period, were cushioned, at least to some degree, by the island's agricultural base. This is reflected in the economic statistics for 2013 quoted earlier, in which Crete's GDP was the fourth highest in the country. However, the impact on the island's economy and its people's livelihoods was still very serious. Although relatively high by Greek standards, its GDP was only 63% of the European average.[111]

The economic crisis also had a cataclysmic effect on the country's political system. This is reflected in the comment by the country's president reproduced at the beginning of this section, which was made on the 40th anniversary of the restoration of democracy in 1974. Since 1974, there had been two main political parties in Greece, the right-wing New Democracy and left-wing PASOK, and they had alternated in power. However, the economic crisis led to the rise of a new opposition party, the Coalition of the Radical Left (SYRIZA). SYRIZA's success was due to its opposition to the austerity reforms. It maintained that, instead of agreeing to the Troika's package of loans and reforms, the government should have negotiated the cancellation or rescheduling of the country's debts. Most of its support came from people who previously would have voted for PASOK, which was blamed for the country's problems because it was in power at the time of the economic collapse and negotiated the bail-out.

2012 was a year of political chaos. There were two general elections. In the first, New Democracy gained the most votes but SYRIZA came a very close second. Neither New Democracy nor SYRIZA had enough votes to form a government on their own and, although both tried to form a coalition with other parties, their efforts failed. Consequently, a second election had to be held. The results were much the same, but this time New Democracy and PASOK agreed to form a coalition, thus leaving SYRIZA as the main opposition party.

For the next two years, there was relative stability under the coalition government. However, SYRIZA continued to gain support, winning the largest number of votes in the 2014 European elections, and in December 2014 a new crisis emerged. Greece has a non-executive president who is elected by parliament, not by the general public. However, the candidate, who is nominated by the ruling party, has to be approved by a two-thirds majority of members. If he or she is not approved, a general election has to be called. In December 2014, the government's candidate failed to achieve the necessary number of votes and so an election was held the following month.

The January 2015 election was a momentous event, not just for Greece but for Europe as a whole. SYRIZA achieved a resounding victory, polling 36% of the votes against New Democracy's 28%. A militant far-right party, Golden Dawn, came third – a result that caused not only concern but also surprise, since its leaders were in prison under a charge of attempted murder at the time. SYRIZA's win gave it 149 seats in parliament, which was two less than the 151 needed for an outright majority. However, this time it had no problem in forming a coalition; it joined forces with a small right-wing party, the Independent Greeks. Thus, on 26 January 2015 SYRIZA's leader, Alexis Tsipras, became prime minister.

However, Tsipras' victory at home was only the first of the battles he had to fight, since he then had to face the EU and the IMF. He had to convince them to write off some of Greece's debt, approve his government's proposed policy of socialist growth rather than neoliberal austerity, and lend him some more money to tide him over the initial transition period. This proved to be a much more difficult task than winning the elections.

By this time, the country's economic and political problems had changed its relationship with Brussels. The EU's role had been transformed from one of benevolent partner in economic growth to that of ruthless moneylender, imposing poverty and hardship in return for crippling loans. During the bail-out period, the Troika did not just impose economic and administrative policies, but also 'micromanaged' their implementation. Moreover, it also attempted to influence the country's internal politics. The crux came in the run-up to the presidential elections in December 2014, when Jean-Claude Juncker, the president of the European Commission, stated publically that he supported the government's candidate and that, should elections be necessary, he would like to see 'known faces' rather than 'extreme forces' in power.[112]

Juncker's comments caused a political uproar in Greece. The reasons for his concerns, although not actually stated, were fairly obvious and shared by many EU politicians and officials. He was afraid that, if SYRIZA came to power, not only would Greece fail to pay its debts (most of which were by then to Eurozone governments) or continue its reform programme, but also that this would trigger similar reactions in other member states. However, by making his views public, he was interfering in the internal politics of what was supposed to be a sovereign nation. Moreover, his choice of words was unfortunate, because the term 'extreme forces' could also refer to the militant far-right party, Golden Dawn.

When SYRIZA came to power, Juncker was forced to curb his tongue and during the subsequent negotiations with the new SYRIZA government, he emerged as one of the more moderate players. The main adversary became Germany, which had most to lose, primarily because it had been the main financier of Greece's bail-out loans, but also because of its substantial investment in Greece, much of which, as we have seen, was related to the previous government's privatisation programme – a programme that had been forced upon the government by the Troika and that SYRIZA wished to halt and possibly even reverse.

At the time of writing, the negotiations between Greece and Brussels had been going on for nearly five months and there was still no end in sight. The Greek government offered to make many concessions, but nothing seemed enough to satisfy its creditors. During this time, the economic situation worsened, fuelled by uncertainty and a fear that Greece might be forced to leave the Eurozone, and since the government was running out of money it had to cut public expenditure even further. And as the tensions increased, the confrontation became one of the biggest challenges that either the modern Greek government or the Eurozone had ever had to face.

Whatever the outcome of this unfortunate process, two points of interest emerged during the negotiations. One was that, despite the ill-feeling between Greece and Brussels, most people, in Greece as a whole and in Crete, seemed to want to stay not just in the EU but also in the Eurozone. This was in line with SYRIZA's policy, which had always been to reform the EU and Greece's relationship with it, not to leave it. The question was at what cost they were prepared to stay. Neither the people nor the government could afford to accept further austerity.

The second point was that the government gained public respect for confronting the EU. Four months after the election, when the economy had begun to be badly affected and people were beginning to despair of a solution, an opinion poll found that 48.5%

of the population supported SYRIZA, substantially more than in the election, while New Democracy's support had fallen to 21%. And 77% of those polled had confidence in Alexis Tsipras.[113] I share this respect. Greece has challenged many of the EU's weaknesses: its economic policies, the feasibility of a common currency, the lack of democracy and decentralisation, and the increasing dominance of Germany.

International

The establishment of a global system of governance has lagged behind the social and economic dimensions of globalisation. It is therefore not surprising that in Greece, as elsewhere, international agencies have relatively little impact on day-to-day activities – certainly much less than those of the EU. However, their presence is still felt. The most obvious example, perhaps, is the IMF, which joined forces with the European Central Bank to fund Greece's bail-out programme. Another case, to which brief mention has already been made, relates to refugees. Greece has had to follow international regulations regarding the treatment of refugees, and has also received considerable support from organisations such as the UN High Commission for Refugees and the International Office of Migration. A third, and rather different, example is the role of international agencies in monitoring social conditions in the country, particularly during the aftermath of the 2008 economic crisis, when both the International Labour Organisation and Oxfam published reports drawing attention to the impact of the austerity measures on the lives of ordinary Greek people.[114]

Furthermore, because of its strategic location in the eastern Mediterranean, Crete itself has continued to play an important role in international politics. For example, during the Cold War, a number of United States and NATO military bases were established on the island. Most have since been closed, but there is still a small US naval support base at Souda Bay, near Chania in western Crete. And in 2014, nuclear weapons confiscated from Syria were decontaminated on board a ship just off Crete's western coast, before being shipped to Italy and thence to the UK for disposal. Although in these cases there was no overt military force, one cannot help being reminded of earlier occasions when Crete was used as a battleground between international powers – for example, between the Venetians and the Turks in the 17th century, or the allied powers and Germany in the Second World War.

Impact of political domination

We have seen in this section that Crete has lost its sovereignty, not only to Greece but also to the EU and to some extent to global powers, and we have also seen that this has had both positive and negative effects. However, the lack of protest from Cretans suggests that, at least in their eyes, the benefits have outweighed the costs. The island has benefited from Greece's periods of economic success and from the positive aspects of its membership of the EU, and has not suffered as much as many other parts of the country from the negative side of the story. Moreover, one could argue that, as an integral part of Greece rather than an independent entity, Crete has not had to take responsibility, administratively, financially or politically, for either engineering the successes or dealing with the problems. Whether this situation continues indefinitely, and what Crete will do if it changes, remains to be seen.

Conclusion

The invasion of Crete described in this chapter may at first sight seem very different from those of the past. In fact, some critics might question the appropriateness of my use of the term 'invasion'. However, I would argue that there are in fact many similarities. In order to make my point, I will identify four possible arguments that these critics might put forward and discuss their validity.

The first argument they might make is that one cannot compare the present situation with that of the past because Crete is no longer an independent entity. It is true that Crete is now part of Greece and, as I warned in Chapter 1, this means that it is sometimes difficult to distinguish between the situation in Crete and that in Greece as a whole. However, this is not a new problem. As we saw in Chapter 3, Crete's links with Greece go back a long way. From the end of the Minoan civilisation around 1450 BC until the advent of the Romans in the first century BC, it was directly under Greek influence; and for most of the rest of its history, it was subject to the same external power as other parts of what is now Greece, the main exception being the Venetian era. The difference between then and now is not the status of Crete but the nature of the larger political entity of which it is or was part. It is now part of the Greek nation state. However, nation states are relatively recent phenomena; in the past, political entities tended to be weaker and less clearly defined. Moreover, as we have seen in this chapter, it is also part of a larger and more nebulous political body, the European Union, which is not unlike some of the earlier empires.

The second argument my critics might pose is that the current 'invasion' has not occurred suddenly. It has been a gradual process of change, and one that is still ongoing. However, one of the main conclusions drawn in Chapter 3 was that very few if any of the previous invasions had clear beginnings or endings. There were a number of key dates, such as those of the first Roman invasion, the Turkish withdrawal from specific parts of the island, the unification of Crete with Greece, and the German invasion of Chania, but these were merely milestones along the road of change. One can identify similar milestones today; for example, the dates when Greece joined the EU and the Eurozone, the times when there were marked increases or decreases in the number of tourists in Crete, the date when the memorandum with the Troika was signed, and the key elections of 2012 and 2015. Between these milestones, the process of change, now as in the past, has been gradual.

A third argument might be that the changes taking place now are primarily economic and social rather than political; there has been no use of military force and (except in the sense that Crete is now governed from Athens) no takeover of government. There are two main counter-arguments to this point. Firstly, another of the conclusions in Chapter 3 was that the earlier invasions were much more than takeovers of political power. They were multi-faceted, involving movements of people and goods and the exchange of ideas and culture and affecting all aspects of the island's society.

Secondly, although there has been no military intervention or formal takeover of government in the current invasion, the economic and political policies imposed upon Greece (and thus upon Crete) by the EU, and to a lesser extent by global governance agencies, have certainly affected the country's sovereignty. During the bail-out period the Troika's impact was so great that one could argue that in many respects it was the government. And the battle of wills between the 'Brussels Group' (as the Troika was euphemistically renamed in the course of the negotiations) and Greece's new SYRIZA government in 2015 was as tough as any military conflict. In fact, one might liken it to a siege, in that the Brussels Group's tactic was to force Greece to surrender by starving it of cash. Moreover, one might also compare the role of the Brussels Group with that of the four Great Powers in the 19th century, while Germany's dominant role in the negotiations has brought back memories in Greece of the German occupation in the Second World War.

The fourth possible argument is that this cannot be called an 'invasion' because the Cretan people have benefited and appear to have been willing collaborators rather than either victims or protagonists. Here there are three main counter-arguments. Firstly, we saw in Chapter 3 that in the previous invasions there were benefits as well as costs. Secondly, there is an element of victimisation in the present invasion, in the sense that Cretans have suffered from events that have been beyond their control or not of their own choosing, such as decisions made by the Greek government or the EU. The third counter-argument concerns the nature of the Cretans' response, which is the subject of the next chapter. I will argue there that their response to this invasion is very similar to that in the past. We will see that now, as in the past, Cretans are exploiting opportunities for their own gain and collaborating when it is in their interests to do so, but that they are also resisting those aspects of the invasion that they resent or consider not in their interests. The critical question has always been at what point the Cretans decide that 'enough is enough' and thus begin to resist rather than tolerate or collaborate and we shall see that this is still the case today.

Chapter 5

The Cretan Response: Let's Make the Most of It

> On two things every traveller and historian is agreed:
> the bravery of the people and the beauty of the island.
> (Michael Llewellyn Smith, *Crete: The Great Island*,
> Longman, 1965, p.12)

In the previous chapter, I mentioned a Greek friend from the UK who came to Crete in 2014 to visit her niece and nephew, who were studying here. My friend, whom I will refer to as Marina, is from the mainland and, since it was her first visit to Crete, I was interested to hear her reactions. It was the height of the tourist season when she visited and she was impressed by the way in which the Cretans dealt with the massive influx of tourists. She was impressed not only by the efficient way in which services, such as hotels, restaurants and buses, operated, but also by the attitude of the service providers, who appeared to combine efficiency with an air of nonchalance and a wry sense of humour.

Her comments about people's attitudes interested me because I had gained the same impression. In Crete, as elsewhere, it is difficult to generalise about people's behaviour. There are always some people who go out of their way to provide a good service and some who do not, some who are friendly and some who are not. Nevertheless, I sensed something distinctive about the Cretan attitude. I had a feeling that the Cretans have learned how to provide an efficient service while at the same time protecting their own interests and maintaining their dignity and self-esteem. This is reflected in their approach to work, which is to do what is necessary without killing oneself in the process. And it is reflected in their attitude not just to tourists but to any 'outsider', which might best be described as a good-natured but at times somewhat condescending tolerance. I can imagine a Cretan saying: 'They are a weird lot, these foreigners, and they can be a real pain at times. But we value their custom so we put up with them.'

One might argue that this approach is common in any society where people are dependent on mass tourism for their livelihood. However, I suspected that in this case it reflected something more profound. I had a hunch that the Cretans' response to the latest 'invasion' stemmed, at least in part, from their past history. And Marina's comments were important, not just because they supported my hypothesis but also because, as a Greek, her observations were in some respects more valid than mine. She was not treated in the same way as foreign tourists and, since she spoke Greek, she could understand what the local people were saying. It was also significant that she noted differences between Crete and the mainland.

In this chapter, I will expand my argument. I will seek to explain the various ways in which the Cretan people have reacted to the contemporary invasion, and I will attempt to show that these reactions are in many respects similar to their responses to earlier ones. At the end of Chapter 3, I identified three common characteristics regarding the Cretans' response to these earlier invasions. Firstly, they used the invasions to their advantage, exploiting any economic and political opportunities that arose and adopting some social innovations and cultural practices. Secondly, they nevertheless managed to retain their own social and cultural identity and a sense of pride and self-esteem. And thirdly, they either ignored or resisted any aspects of the invasion that were not in their interests. Let us look at each of these three points and see how relevant they are today.

Exploitation of Opportunities

> Much of the beauty of Crete is that it is a *cultural land-scape*. (Rackham, O. and J. Moody, *The Making of the Cretan Landscape*, Manchester University Press, p.xi.)

We saw in the previous chapter that, as in previous invasions, Crete has benefited in many ways, especially in terms of economic development. The most obvious example is tourism, but there have also been benefits from other forms of trade and investment, from migration and from the union with Greece and Greece's membership of the EU. These benefits cannot be attributed merely to good fortune. It is not simply that Crete has been in the right place at the right time. Cretans have, as in the past, made the most of the situation. They have done so in four main ways: through investment, by utilising the island's resources, by playing their political cards well, and through sheer hard work.

Investment

We saw in Chapter 4 that the current invasion has resulted in substantial external investment in Crete - from other parts of Greece, from other EU countries and from the rest of the world. However, Cretans have also invested. They have invested not only money but also effort and ingenuity. This is particularly evident in the case of tourism. A successful tourist industry requires financial investment, initiative and organisation and the Cretan contribution has been significant. It can be divided into two main types: private and public.

Private investment includes things like accommodation, restaurants, shops, travel agents, and transport facilities, in all of which there is local as well as external investment. For example, in the case of accommodation, there are many small, locally-owned places to stay, including hotels, self-catering apartments and rooms. In recent years, an increase in the number of large hotels, both Greek and foreign-owned, has forced some of these out of business. However, the large number of small establishments remains one of Crete's attractions. The same is true of restaurants and tourist shops, while in the case of transport there are local as well as externally-owned coach and car hire companies. Moreover, the main bus company, KTEL, although operating nationwide, is highly decentralised. Its regional branches (of which there are two in Crete, one serving the west and one the east) are locally-managed and sufficiently autonomous to be able to adapt to meet local patterns of demand.

Public investment includes services such as the upkeep of roads, airports and beaches, immigration, air traffic control, police and refuse collection, all of which have to be maintained to a high standard and expanded to cope with the vast increase in demand during the tourist season. Some of these, such as major roads, airports and police, are the responsibility of the central government, but others, including refuse collection and the maintenance of local roads, town centres and beaches, are local authority functions.

Spring is a good time to appreciate the extent of this investment, both private and public. As the start of the tourist season approaches, there is a hive of activity. Hotel and restaurant owners redecorate or extend their premises, shopkeepers restock their shelves, car hire companies replenish and service their fleets, and KTEL commissions extra buses and introduces its expanded summer timetable, which in Aghios Nikolaos includes a local tourist route. Meanwhile, the local authorities repair and repaint the toilets and showers on the beaches, bring out the sunbeds and sunshades, and smarten up the town centres.

There is also a special effort to cater for the particular needs of the various types of tourist, especially in terms of language. Most of the official information that tourists are likely to need, such as road signs, transport schedules, and information in museums and at archaeological sites, is written in English as well as in Greek, and most shops and restaurants advertise their wares in several foreign languages, especially English and German but often also Russian and sometimes French. Most people working in the tourist industry speak reasonable English and many one or more other foreign language as well. The importance of Russian tourists is now widely recognised and many people have already learnt some Russian, while others express the wish to do so. Maybe there will soon be a demand to learn Chinese?

The standard of services, both private and public, is, as my friend Marina noted, generally high. Some aspects of service provision do not always quite meet northern European standards. The most obvious examples relate to sanitary facilities. In many smaller hotels and self-catering apartments, there are no proper shower cubicles so the water goes all over the floor and in both hotels and public toilets there is the unpleasant requirement (due, one is told, to the capacity of the sewage systems) to put toilet paper in a receptacle instead of down the toilet. The attitude of some staff could also perhaps be better. In hotels, shops and restaurants, the vast majority of staff are polite and friendly and make the visitor feel welcome. But in some other services, such as buses and government offices, there is a tendency to be brusque, sometimes almost to the point of rudeness. It is on occasions like these that one gets the feeling that outsiders are in fact tolerated rather than welcomed.

However, these are minor issues. One seldom hears tourists complain about the quality of services and my own experience has also been good. When travelling by bus, I have always managed to reach my destination without any major mishap and I have only once stayed in a hotel or apartment that was unsatisfactory and never had a bad meal in a restaurant. The quality of food warrants special mention. It is one of the main attractions not only for tourists but also for long-term residents. Expatriate residents seldom invite friends to their homes for a meal; they invite them to a local *taverna*.

Another example of local investment and ingenuity is the expatriate property market. Estate agents are a relatively new phenomenon in Crete, and one created primarily for the expatriate market. Most exchanges of property between local people are undertaken by word of mouth or through advertisements in local newspapers. However, when the property market began to boom, estate agents specialising in the sale of property to expatriates sprung up in all the main towns and, although they were severely hit by the crash in the property market, many still operate today.

These agencies are tailor-made for the expatriate market. They provide a comprehensive service, including introducing the client to a lawyer and a notary (in Greece, the two roles are different but each lawyer seems to have his or her own notary and the two work as a team), helping them open a bank account and register with the tax office (both of which are legal requirements for anyone buying property) and, after the sale, undertaking any necessary renovations or extensions or, in cases where the client buys vacant land, designing and building their house. Such assistance is a godsend for would-be buyers, most of whom are not resident in the country at the time and, in particular, do not speak Greek. Many of these agencies employ non-Greek residents to help liaise with the clients.

Utilisation of resources

Crete has also made maximum use of its resources, both natural and human. Tourism again provides the most obvious example of this. The island's natural resources alone would be enough to attract tourists, with its beautiful coastline, spectacular mountain scenery and long hot summers. However, it also has a fascinating history, of which evidence abounds, and a vibrant culture. Manifestations of the latter range from the picturesque villages nestled on valley sides and little white-painted churches perched on the top of hills, to the traditional food, dancing and crafts, and the ubiquitous street cafés, which help to create the image of Crete as a relaxed, laid-back place - and thus a good place to visit.

As I mentioned in Chapter 2, I spent a month in New Zealand soon after moving to Crete. It was my first visit to the country and, like most visitors, I was impressed by its spectacular scenery. I spent most of the time in the South Island, where the combination of beautiful coastline and awesome mountains reminded me of Crete. However, when I returned, I realised that Crete has something that New Zealand lacks: the history and, in particular, the culture. New Zealand has some interesting recent history and some nice small towns and villages; but it was (as far as we know) uninhabited until the 13th century and even now the population density is very low. One can travel many miles without seeing any sign of human habitation - other than perhaps a few sheep. Crete, on the other hand, is, as Rackham and Moody point out in the quotation at the beginning of this section, 'a cultural landscape'.

Cretans have made it very easy for tourists to enjoy these assets. In order to demonstrate this, I will describe three possible days in the life of a tourist based in Aghios Nikolaos, which, as I noted in Chapter 4, is an excellent base from which to tour the eastern part of the island. The itineraries I will describe are based on those I have actually undertaken with friends who have visited me here.

On the first day, we will drive up to the nearby village of Kritsa. We will make two stops on the way. The first will be at the little Byzantine church known as Panagia Kera, which is known in particular for its frescoes. The second will be at the remains of the ancient Greek town of Lato, which is the best preserved Doric town on the island and commands spectacular views over the surrounding countryside. In Kritsa itself, we will have a light *meze* lunch at one of my favourite *tavernas*, and then explore the fascinating narrow village streets and browse through the craft shops. We will return to Aghios Nikoloas in time either to do some souvenir shopping or to relax at one of the town's many small sandy beaches, and then round off the day with a meal at a restaurant overlooking the mysterious Lake Voulismeni.

On the second day, we will venture further afield. We will drive to the southern coastal town of Ierapetra, stopping on the way at the remains of the old Minoan town of Gournia, which is one of the best-preserved Minoan sites. After a brief stop for coffee in Ierapetra, we will drive along the coast to the little village of Myrtos, which (as I mentioned in Chapter 4) attracts a rather different type of tourist. There we can have a swim in the warm Libyan sea and lunch at either a seafront restaurant or a *taverna* in the village centre.

If we have time, we might also visit the little village museum, which a friend and I discovered by accident when wandering through the village one day. Many Cretan villages have their own museums, established and run by local people, and the one in Myrtos has a particularly interesting history. In the 1960s, the village school teacher, Georgos Dimitrianakis, discovered some artefacts at a site near Myrtos called Pyrgos. He drew them to the attention of a visiting English archaeologist, Peter Warren, who excavated the site in 1970-71 and found the remains of a significant Minoan settlement. Interestingly, one of the members of Warren's team was Oliver Rackham, co-author of *The Making of the Cretan Landscape*. It was his first visit to Crete. The museum was established by Dimitrianakis and, after his death in 1994, was taken over by the local council. It is currently run by an elderly Englishman who has lived in the village for many years. Most of the exhibits relate to the Pyrgos site and one of the showpieces is a table-top model of the settlement, made by the Englishman.

We will return to Aghios Nikolaos by a more mountainous route, stopping at a lookout where there are spectacular views of both the north and south coasts, and then for a cup of tea or coffee or a drink at the picturesque village of Kalamafka. If we have enough energy, which is perhaps unlikely by this time, we can climb the

224 steps to the Timios Taurus chapel, which is built in a cave in the side of a hill overlooking the village. In the evening, we will eat at one of the many seafront restaurants in or near Aghios Nikolaos.

On the third day, we will drive to the nearby village of Elounda and take the short boat trip to the little rocky island of Spinalonga. As we saw in Chapter 3, Spinalonga has a fascinating history. In the Minoan era, it was used to protect the now-submerged coastal town of Olous; in Venetian times it was an important fortress, which held out against the Turks for nearly fifty years after the rest of Crete was captured; it then became a major Turkish settlement and trading centre; and finally, between 1904 and 1957, it was a leper colony. This last phase of its history is featured in *The Island*, a well-known novel by Victoria Hislop which was published in 2005 and later filmed for television.[115] This book has made Spinalonga famous and explains much of its popularity as a tourist destination. However, the island is a fascinating place to visit for other reasons. Since both the Venetian fortifications and Turkish buildings (which were used by the lepers) can still be seen, it provides a microcosm of Cretan history.

After an hour or so exploring the island, we will return to Elounda for lunch at one of the many seafront restaurants. We can then either relax on its pleasant sandy beach or drive over the mountains to the inland town of Neapoli, which was once the administrative centre of the region. Neapoli is an interesting place to visit, partly because of its maze of little streets and squares but also because it is not a tourist town so one gets some idea of ordinary daily life. In the evening, we will drive to a village called Exo Lakonia, a few miles out of Aghios Nikolaos, and eat in a well-known *taverna* that provides some of the best traditional food in the area, served in traditional style and at a remarkably low price.

These are only three of innumerable possible itineraries, all of which effortlessly combine the attractions of Crete's natural environment with those of its history and culture. It is these attractions that also make Crete a popular place to come not just to visit but to live - at least for much of the year; we shall see in the next chapter that life in winter is very different. In these particular cases, it is assumed that the visitor (or resident) has access to a vehicle. However, one can visit many of the places mentioned, including Panagia Kera and Kritsa, Gournia and Myrtos, and Elounda, Spinalonga and Neapoli, by public transport. It takes a little longer, but the journeys themselves are interesting experiences, in which one gets a taste of local life.

Another important way in which Crete has made the most of its resources is by maintaining the importance of agriculture. Agriculture has always been a mainstay of the economy. Throughout the island's history it has played a very important role, both as a means of subsistence and as a basis for trade and commerce. The principal crop is (and always has been) olives, which are grown primarily for their oil. Crete is one of the main producers of olive oil in the world and its oil is known for its exceptionally high quality. As I mentioned in Chapter 2, there are olive groves everywhere in Crete. Although some of these are neglected and others used only for subsistence purposes, most provide a source of income. We also saw in Chapter 2 that the island produces a wide variety of vegetables and fruit. Again, some of the produce is used for subsistence purposes but much is sold commercially, both locally in Crete and to the mainland and other parts of Europe.

In many parts of the world, the development of a new source of income, such as mining, manufacturing industry or tourism, has been the death-knell for agriculture. But this has not been the case in Crete. Tourism and agriculture actually complement each other well. An obvious example is that vegetables and fruit supply the tourist industry, while olive oil products are an important tourist attraction. Equally if not more important, however, is agriculture's role as an alternative source of livelihood. I mentioned in Chapter 4 that the island's agricultural base helped its people to survive the recession that followed the 2008 financial crisis. Agriculture provided not only an alternative source of income but also a means of subsistence. Most Cretans have access, directly or indirectly, to some land, and so they were at least able to get food. Moreover, it is also a source of livelihood in winter, when there is no tourist income.

In this respect, the seasonality of both activities is a positive factor. The main agricultural activities, especially the olive harvest, occur in winter, and when the tourist season is over, many urban dwellers disappear to the rural areas to harvest their olive crops. Winter is also a time to rest and recuperate after the busy tourist season. The length of the tourist season is gradually increasing in Crete and some people believe that winter tourism should be better promoted. However, given the importance of winter for other activities, one cannot help wondering whether this would really be such a good thing.

Crete has not only maintained its agricultural base, but also developed it in response to the changing external environment. In the case of olives, for example, it has taken advantage of Italy's demand for high quality oil to blend with some of its lower quality produce and of EU subsidies. And in the case of vegetables, it has promoted the use of plastic greenhouses (or polytunnels), which were apparently introduced to the Ierapetra area by a Dutchman in the 1950s. Crete is reputed to have half the greenhouses in Greece,[116] and most of these are in Ierapetra. The area is served by a network of small farm roads and an irrigation system that pipes water from a large dam in the hills above. Some of the produce is sold locally, but much is exported to the mainland and to other parts of Europe.

The export of olives and vegetables also demonstrates the way in which Crete has exploited its trade opportunities. Its location is no longer as critical as it was in previous eras, except perhaps as an occasional forced landing point for refugees and illegal migrants travelling by boat from Turkey to Italy. However, trade is still important. Of particular interest is the growing trade with Russia. I mentioned in Chapter 4 the increasing quantities of fruit and vegetables exported there. A less obvious example, and one that exemplifies Cretan ingenuity, is the sale of fur clothing to Russian tourists. Non-Russian visitors to Crete are often surprised by the many shops selling fur goods. Who would want to buy furs in this climate, they ask? The answer is the Russians. The goods are apparently imported from an area in northern Greece that specialises in the manufacture of fur products.

Playing the political game

Cretans have also exploited the situation by playing their political cards well. As we have seen in previous chapters, there have been strong links between Cretan and Greek politics since the days of Eleftherios Venizelos, the Cretan politician who went on to become prime minister of Greece. Since Crete's union with Greece, its politicians have not just sat back and relaxed, accepting whatever fortune might befall them. They have participated actively in Greek politics and used not only their membership of Greece but also Greece's membership of the EU to their own benefit and, in general, that of the island as a whole.

In order to understand how they have done this, one needs to know how the political system works. Greece, including Crete, has what one might call a 'patronage-based' or 'clientelistic' political culture; that is, one in which politicians gain political support by providing (or at least promising to provide) benefits to individuals or local areas. In other words, people tend to vote for someone not because of the policies that they or their party advocates, but because of the personal benefits they have promised them – or, in some cases, the personal damage they might do to them if they don't support them. There are elements of patronage in all political systems. The important question is how big a role it plays, and in Greece its role is quite significant.

Crete's patronage system is deeply rooted in the traditional structure of its society. We saw in Chapter 3 that Cretan society has, since the latter part of the Byzantine era, been dominated (socially, economically and politically) by a relatively small number of powerful extended families; and this is typical of Greece as a whole. The system is very similar to that on which the Italian *mafia* is based. As in Italy, the family heads are often known as godfathers; the Greek word is *νονοί*, which is pronounced 'nonie'. In fact, in Greece these men often really are godfathers in the original sense of the word, and this is one of the ways in which they exert their influence. They 'buy' people's support by offering to become their child's godfather.

In patronage-based systems, people tend to vote for candidates whom they know and with whom they or their families have some sort of personal ties, and so the same politicians, and thus the same parties, get elected over and over again. This has been the case in Greece. The two main parties that dominated Greek politics between 1974 and 2012, New Democracy and PASOK, were each dominated by a powerful extended family: New Democracy by the Karamanlis family and PASOK by the Papandreou family. During this period, Crete became a battleground once again. In this case, the battles were not between international powers but between Greece's two main political parties, but they were nevertheless heated and they had a significant effect on the island's economic and political status.

The island's voters originally supported New Democracy. This was due primarily to the influence of Kostas Mitsotakis, a member of one of its most powerful political families, who was the leader of New Democracy from 1984 to 1993 and prime minister from 1990 to 1993. However, when PASOK was in power, it made a special effort to woo Cretan voters by providing them with material benefits, including privileged access to the spoils of EU membership, such as agricultural subsidies and infrastructure projects. Cretan politicians and entrepreneurs were willing collaborators in this process. For example, in the case of agricultural subsidies, they submitted false agricultural data (such as gross overestimates of the numbers of olive trees and livestock) to the government, which in turn submitted them knowingly to the authorities in Brussels.[117] And in return, they showed their appreciation by voting for PASOK. By the end of the period, Crete had become a strong PASOK supporter. As a friend put it, the map of Crete was green – a reference to the fact that PASOK's traditional colour is green.

However, in 2010 SYRIZA's rise to power began and the political map of Crete, like that of the country as a whole, began to change. SYRIZA's political success was significant, not only because of its opposition to the bail-out agreement but also because it was not backed by any of the powerful traditional families and so constituted a challenge to patronage politics. In Crete, as elsewhere, support for PASOK collapsed, while that for SYRIZA increased dramatically. In the 2012 elections, SYRIZA gained 32% of the island's votes, while New Democracy came second with 22%; PASOK received only 18%. Three years later, the 2015 elections saw SYRIZA's share of the votes rise to 45%. New Democracy's share remained much the same, but support for PASOK fell to around 5%. Interestingly, however, the militant far-right party, Golden Dawn, got very few votes in Crete. I will discuss the implications of these results later.

Although our main concern is with Crete, it should be noted that Greece has also played the political game. For example, it appears not only that the PASOK government was aware of the manipulation of agricultural statistics in Crete, but that this was only one of a number of cases when the quality of the statistics that Greece presented to the EU was somewhat dubious. In 2004 it was revealed that when Greece entered the Eurozone, its deficit had exceeded the official EU limit, but this had been ignored, partly because part of the deficit was blamed on the costs of hosting the 2002 Olympic Games but also because the Greek government had manipulated some of the figures.[118]

More recently and, one could argue, more creditably, during the negotiations between Greece and the EU after the 2015 elections, the Greek government played a number of strategic cards. For example, it exposed the weaknesses in Germany's position, including not only its interests in Greece's privatisation programme and the corruption scandals, but also the analogies between Germany's present position in Europe and that during the Second World War. It even reopened a long-standing dispute over the payment of reparations for war damage. It also opened discussions with both Russia and China over future trade and investment links and even possible loans and threatened to veto continued EU sanctions against Russia. And, of course, it made the most of the widespread fears in the Eurozone about the wider repercussions of a 'Grexit' – the term used to refer to Greece's exit from the currency union.

Hard work

> A huge customs officer was smoking a hookah in the customs shed. [...] He slowly raised the hookah tube and said in a sleepy voice: 'Welcome!'
> One of the urchins came up to me. He winked with his olive-black eyes and said in a mocking tone:
> 'He's no Cretan. He's a lazy devil.'
> 'Aren't Cretans lazy devils too?'
> 'They are... yes, they are,' the young Cretan replied, 'but in a different way'.
> (Nikos Kazantzakis, *Zorba the Greek*, Faber and Faber, 1952, p.28)

Last but not least, Cretans have exploited the opportunities that the latest invasion has provided through sheer hard work. This may surprise some people, since Cretans, and Greeks as a whole, are sometimes regarded as being at best 'laid-back' and at worst lazy. The above quotation from *Zorba the Greek* suggests that this was the case in Nikos Kazantazakis' time, and it is still common today. It was a sore point during the conflicts with the EU, when some people made comparisons between the 'lazy Greeks' and the 'hard-working Germans'.

One of the factors that contribute to this image today is the 'street-café culture'. I mentioned earlier that Crete's cultural attractions include the large number of street cafés. One cannot walk more than a few metres down any street in a town or village without coming across such a café. They have evolved from the *kafeneion* or coffee shops, which were an essential element of traditional Greek society. They have tables inside as well as on the pavement outside, but unless the weather is very bad, most people sit outside. A range of alcoholic and non-alcoholic drinks and snacks is usually available, but the most popular drink is still coffee. These cafés are not simply places to come for a quick drink. They are also social centres and meeting places. People come to chat, discuss local or national events, play board games, and sometimes watch television. These cafes are always well patronised, and this creates an image that Cretans have nothing better to do than sit and drink coffee and chat all day.

However, as the quotation from *Zorba the Greek* also suggests, this image can be misleading. Cretan people know how to relax, but they also know how to work and, if they have to work, they do so. During the tourist season in particular, people work very long hours, not just in the hotels but in all the other related activities. Shops and restaurants are open from early in the morning until late at night, seven days a week. Transport services also operate round the clock, since the flights that bring the tourists arrive at all hours of the day and night. And local authority staff work at night to clear the vast quantities of rubbish left on the streets and beaches.

In the case of the street cafes, the employees work extremely hard and many patrons merely drop in for a quick cup of coffee before or after work. Most of those who sit there all day are either elderly or unemployed, and the latter are idle not by choice but because of the high level of unemployment. Since many of these people are not well off, a single cup of coffee is often made to last several hours.

Retention of Identity and Self-Esteem

> Although it could not be more Greek, Crete is really a country within a country, with its own history, folklore and traditions. (*Crete*, Dorling Kindersley, Eyewitness Travel Top 10 Travel Guides, 2005, p.6).

The second characteristic of the Cretans' response to previous invasions was that they managed to retain those aspects of their way of life that were important to them and thus to retain their identity and self-esteem. In this section, I will attempt to show that this is the same today. I will argue that it is reflected in five main aspects of life: economy, language, religion, culture and political identity.

Economy

Although the rise of tourism and other forms of external investment have in many respects transformed the Cretan economy, some aspects of the traditional mode of life remain. This is most evident in the case of agriculture. Although commercial agriculture has developed in response to new demands and technology, subsistence agricultural practices have changed remarkably little over the centuries. In fact, in many respects, they are not unlike those practised by the early Minoan farmers. As I mentioned in Chapter 2, in addition to olives, people cultivate a range of food crops, grow fruit trees, and keep sheep, goats and poultry and the occasional pig. Bee-keeping also continues to be an important activity. Many livestock are now kept permanently in pens, either adjacent to people's houses or on small rural plots that the owners visit periodically. However, traditional grazing practices are still common. These include the herding of livestock from one place to another during the day and the seasonal movement of animals between high and low altitudes.

In the area where I live, which is on the outskirts of town, the importance of subsistence agriculture is very evident. Many of my neighbours have some olive trees and fruit trees, grow vegetables and keep a few chickens and the odd goat. And if I venture a little further afield, I often come across small plots of cultivated land, enclosures with a few sheep and goats, usually guarded by a dog, or a cluster of brightly painted wooden beehives, all of which are presumably owned by people living in the town. The sound of the bells that sheep and goats wear when grazing freely is one of the pleasures of my winter walks and sometimes I meet the shepherd. These shepherds are not, as one might expect, young boys or biblical type characters, but ordinary-looking middle-aged or elderly men. One of the most amusing sights I have seen is that of a shepherd grazing his animals along the edge of the new road that was then under construction near my house, carrying on a conversation on his mobile phone! Such anachronisms are very typical of Crete.

Traditional practices are also evident in the retail sector, especially when it comes to food. There are still a large number of small, locally-owned food shops, including specialised ones like bakeries, fishmongers and greengrocers, and every town has a weekly market. Although Cretans are increasingly driven, by economic or time constraints and by the power of the media, to shop in supermarkets like Lidl, they prefer to buy their food in the smaller establishments or at the market, where produce is fresher and sold in a traditional manner - for example, in large barrels or vats, from which customers can select the amount that they want. Bakeries play a particularly important role; Cretans like to buy their bread fresh every day, and from a bakery rather than a supermarket.

Other examples of traditional economic practices include the widespread use of cash and the importance of personal contacts in any form of economic exchange. Most financial transactions are made with cash rather than by cheque or electronic payment, although the latter is becoming more common, and many people keep large sums of cash in their homes. The importance of personal contacts is related to the clientelistic nature of society. I will say more about its effects, which can be both positive and negative, in the next chapter.

Finally, it should be noted that, although Crete's economy is now highly integrated into that of Greece, there is still some sense of local economic identity. I have already mentioned the large number of locally-owned tourist facilities, the decentralisation of the bus company, KTEL, and the many small locally-owned food shops. In addition, the island has its own bank (the Pankreta Bank), its own newspapers and its own television and radio stations.

Language

We saw in Chapter 3 that language has played a major role in unifying the Greek people and that this has had a major effect on the history of Crete, not least in the pressure for unity with Greece. And this is still the case today. Although many people in Crete, especially the younger generation and those involved in tourism and commerce, are able to speak English and sometimes other foreign languages, Greek remains the main language and the language of preference. All official documents are produced in Greek, newspapers and locally-produced television programmes are all in Greek, and people communicate with each other in Greek. In other words, Greek is used as much as, say, French is in France or German in Germany. Moreover, people are proud of their language. Soon after I moved into my apartment, I had a conversation, partly in Greek but mainly in English, with a television technician who had come to install a TV aerial for me. He said it was a great pity that foreigners, and particularly English people, did not make more effort to speak Greek because it is such a rich and beautiful language.

It is interesting to note the aspects of everyday life, other than communication with foreigners, in which English is used rather than Greek. The most obvious uses are in advertising and information technology. However, even in the latter, many English terms (such as computer, email and internet) are transliterated into Greek script. Another example is transport. For example, car registration plates use the Latin rather than Greek alphabet; the trains that run between major towns on the mainland are known as IC (Inter-City) trains, with IC written in Latin script; and on Greek airlines the pilot's instructions to cabin crew to 'take their seats for landing' are issued in English. Maybe the last is an international requirement?

More interesting, however, is the frequent use of English phrases in a political context. In some cases, this merely reflects the foreign origin of a concept. For example, alternative strategies are referred to as 'plan A' and 'plan B' and, of course, when Greece's membership of the Eurozone was under threat, the word 'Grexit' was on everyone's lips. However, English is also used to express a sense of political alienation or frustration. Thus, when the Troika euphemistically referred to Greece's economic reforms, which had brought such hardship to ordinary people, as a 'success story', it was reported *verbatim*; there was no attempt to translate the term into Greek. And English is frequently used in graffiti, which (both in Crete and in Greece as a whole) is ubiquitous and often of very high quality. For example, on a wall overlooking a major road in Aghios Nikolaos someone has painted the word BANKERS, while in the Exarchia district of Athens, an area known for its rebellious character, I found slogans like SMASH TROIKA and SHOULD WE OPEN GOVERNMENTS?

However, as with so many things, the issue of language is complex in Crete, because there are differences between standard modern Greek and that spoken in Crete. These differences are not always immediately apparent to the outsider, partly because one needs some knowledge of the language to appreciate them but also because Cretan Greek is more common among some people (for example, villagers and the elderly) than others. The most obvious difference is in the pronunciation of the letter χ, which Greek textbooks tell you to pronounce like the 'ch' in 'loch', but which the Cretans pronounce 'sh'. This distinction is very evident because one hears it every day in the word όχι, which means 'no'.

Both standard modern Greek and Cretan Greek apparently evolved from a common source: a language known as *Koine* (common) Greek, which was an adaptation of classical Greek used as a *lingua franca* throughout the Greek empire. However, over the years, Cretan Greek has evolved somewhat differently from standard Greek. This appears to be due to a number of factors, including the island's distance from the mainland, influences from the languages of other invading people (particularly the Venetians and Turks), and the incorporation of elements of the language spoken by the Minoans. The Minoan language, which archaeologists and linguists refer to as *Linear A*, is thought to be related to, but slightly different from, that from which classical Greek evolved, which is known as *Linear B*.

Most people refer to the language spoken in Crete as a dialect. However, one source claims that, in 2005, 'after 25 years of petitioning by a dedicated group of Cretan linguists', the EU formally recognised 'that Cretan Greek is not a dialect but a living language and believed to be Europe's oldest living language with roots that stretch back further than Ancient Greek'.[119]

Religion

In Chapter 3 we saw that the Orthodox Church has also played a very important role in the history of Crete and of Greece as a whole, and that this has been another powerful unifying factor. And, as with language, this is still the case today. The vast majority of the population are members of the Orthodox group of churches, which includes the Russian as well as the Greek Orthodox churches. And the headquarters of all the Orthodox churches is still in Constantinople - or Istanbul, as it is now called in most places except Greece. In Greece, Orthodox Christianity is the official religion and the government provides financial support to the Church and approves the appointment of church officials. When SYRIZA came to power in 2015, its intention was to abolish the official link between church and state. However, this had to be put on hold due to strong opposition from its coalition partner.

Because of its different history, the status of the Church in Crete differs slightly from that in the rest of the country. There are various administrative divisions, or 'churches', within the Orthodox group and, while most of Greece belongs to the Church of Greece, Crete has its own Church, responsible directly to the Ecumenical Patriarch in Constantinople. The Church of Crete was formally established in 1900, when Crete was an autonomous state. However, the Church of Crete is, like the Church of Greece, responsible to Athens for secular matters.

Religion plays a very important part in the lives of most Greek people. The *2008 European Social Survey* found that more than 90% of Greek people attended church at some time or other. The only other countries to record similar rates of attendance were Cyprus (another Greek Orthodox country) and Poland.[120] And in 2014, a *Eurobarometer* survey found that religion was held in higher respect in Greece than in any other European country except Cyprus and Malta.[121]

My own observations in Crete support these figures. One of the first things that strikes any visitor is the large number of churches. There are churches everywhere. They vary greatly in size and also in appearance and role. In most villages and small towns, there is one major church, in which services are held regularly. It is usually a large, white building with two main towers. However, there are also many smaller churches, which are really more like chapels. They tend to be much older, simpler in shape, constructed of stone or brick, and often whitewashed. These smaller churches (or chapels) are found throughout the countryside, usually in beautiful but often remote or unlikely locations, such as on the top of a mountain peak or the edge of a beach. Most of them only open once a year, on the day that commemorates the saint after which they are named. There are also many roadside shrines, while some people have shrines outside their house or even a small chapel in their garden.

There appear to be several reasons for the location of these small churches and shrines. One is protection. Thus the churches on beaches are presumably to protect fishermen and the shrines outside people's houses to protect the inhabitants. Another is commemoration. For example, many roadside shrines are on precipitous bends, where there has been an accident. A third reason is access to god. This must be the reason why so many small churches are perched precipitously on the tops of hills. As I mentioned in Chapter 2, there is a long tradition, dating back to Minoan times, of locating places of worship on the tops of hills.

Travelling by bus is a good way to appreciate the nature and extent of religious belief in Crete, since one is able not only to see the many churches and roadside shrines, but also to witness religious practices. Many passengers make the sign of the cross every time the bus passes a church. This is particularly common among older women, but I have also seen many younger people, and even some bus drivers and conductors, do it. The bus drivers are apparently also concerned to ward off evil, since in most buses there is a crucifix and various other religious charms hanging around the driver's seat.

Another manifestation of the importance of religion is the number and importance of religious holidays. If one looks at a list of Greek national holidays, one will find not only that there are a large number but also that there are three different types: secular holidays, such as 25 March, 28 October, Labour Day and New Year's Day; religious holidays that are also secular holidays (i.e. banks, offices, schools, etc. are closed), such as Christmas Day and Easter Sunday; and religious holidays where public facilities remain open - for example, various saints' days. Some of the religious holidays have interesting names, especially when translated into English. For example, the week leading up to Easter (which in English-speaking Christian countries is usually referred to as Holy Week) is known as 'Big Week'. The name of each day of this week is prefaced by the word μεγάλος, which means *big* - Big Monday, Big Tuesday, and so on. Three other examples, all of which are both religious and secular holidays, are Clean Monday (the first Monday in Lent), Good News Day (the Annunciation), and Holy Spirit Monday (Pentecost).

In addition to these nationally recognised holidays, there are local ones. Most towns and villages have a patron saint and their particular saint's day is an official holiday. For example, in Aghios Nikolaos, St Nicholas' Day is an official holiday; public facilities are closed and celebrations are held in the streets. A similar phenomenon is that of 'name days'. Many Greek Christian names are derived from the names of saints, and people with such names celebrate their saint's day, which is referred to as a 'name day', every year. Name days are considered just as important as birthdays, and people (especially children) who don't have a name day (i.e. those not named after a saint) are sometimes considered unfortunate because they only have one annual celebration.

Although most of these religious practices are common to the whole of Greece, there are some differences between Crete and the rest of the country. For example, in Crete Saint Emmanuel's Day is celebrated on 25 December, whereas in the rest of the country it is celebrated on 26 December, and in Crete there are two name days for people named Maria, one for virgins and one for married women! Although these differences are minor, Cretans are proud to point them out.

Religion also continues to play an important role in foreign relations. This is most obvious in the relationship between Greece and Turkey, which is fraught with problems, partly but not only due to the conflict over Cyprus. Greece's persistence in referring to Istanbul as Constantinople is symptomatic of the problem. However, it is also reflected in the relationship between Greece and Russia. The revival of the Orthodox Church in Russia has fostered relations between the two countries and, as I mentioned in Chapter 4, it is one of the factors that attracts Russian tourists to Greece, and in particular to Crete.

Culture

It is difficult to separate religion and culture in Crete, and in Greece as a whole, because they are closely intertwined. Traditional customs and practices have remained surprisingly strong and one of the reasons for this is that they are reinforced by the church.

The importance of religious festivals and name days is an obvious example of this. These occasions are not just religious events but focal aspects of everyday culture and the distinction between religious and secular is blurred. A good example of this   is the celebration that takes place at midnight on Easter Saturday. In the Greek Orthodox Church, Easter (which, incidentally, does not necessarily occur at the same time as in the Catholic or Protestant churches) is considered more important than Christmas and the Saturday night celebration marks the culmination of a week of preparations.

In Aghios Nikolaos the event is held at Lake Voulismeni, the natural lake in the centre of the town. People begin to congregate by the lake from 10 pm onwards. They may have a drink or a meal at one of the lakeside restaurants or just stand and chat. Hawkers wander up and down, selling candles, balloons and other wares, and every now and again someone lets off a fire cracker. Then around 11.30 pm the celebration begins. A candlelit procession emerges from one of the side streets. It is an impressive sight: hundreds of people, all carrying lighted candles, led by priests. The procession comes to a halt by the side of the Lake, where the priests conduct a service. The service is accompanied by a magnificent firework display and culminates in the burning of an effigy of Judas, which is placed on a raft on the Lake. Finally, at midnight, the priests announce (in Greek and, much to my surprise, also in English): 'Christ is Risen!' It is a spectacular event, and a wonderful mixture of religion and pageant – Easter, Guy Fawkes and New Year's Eve all rolled into one!

Another example is the ceremonies that mark key milestones in life: births, marriages and deaths. On one occasion I was invited to a wedding, which turned out to be not just a wedding but also a baptism. The couple had been living together for some time and had a son who was about 15 months old. In this respect, their behaviour was more modern than traditional. However, they wanted the child to be baptised and this would only be possible if they were married. So, like many such couples, they decided to have a joint ceremony: a wedding and then a baptism. Both parts of the ceremony followed traditional custom. For example, at the conclusion of the wedding service, the bride and groom paraded round in a circle while the guests showered them with rice, little bags of which had been provided to everyone. And at the end of the ceremony, all the guests were given some sugared almonds and an almond cookie, both beautifully wrapped. And in the case of the baptism, the little boy was undressed and put right into the font, where he was anointed with water and oil, and afterwards dressed in a smart white suit and tiny boater hat.

Burial practices are also traditional. 'Burial' is not really the right word because the bodies are not actually buried in the ground. They are put in a sarcophagus – a coffin-like construction, usually made of stone, which stands above the ground. I suspect that, like many religious customs throughout the world, this can be attributed more to practicality than to religious belief, since digging graves would be difficult in a rocky place like Crete. Prominent families own their own sarcophagi, to which members of the family are added when they die. But in many cases, the sarcophagus is only rented for three years; the bones are then removed and the sarcophagus is used by someone else. Another interesting practice relates to the publicisation of funerals, which is done by putting notices on lampposts or notice boards in the area where the person lived.

However, burial customs also illustrate the conservative and what many would regard as negative side of religious influence. Not just in Crete but in Greece as a whole, the Church is vehemently opposed to cremation. Legislation allowing for cremation was introduced in 2006, but its implementation was blocked by the church for eight years. A related example is the custom that widows are expected to wear black for the rest of their lives. Although less widely practised than it was, one still sees many older women dressed in black.

The Church's attitude towards women in general is conservative. The most obvious example of this is the absence of any women priests, but it also affects secular life. As in so many societies, the traditional view was that a woman's place is in the home. This attitude is also changing, but much more slowly than in most other European countries. For example, fewer women work, many occupations (including politics) are still dominated by men and older women seldom socialise in public. According to the UNDP's 2013 Human Development Report, Greece ranked 66th out of 187 countries in terms of the percentage of women in parliament (21% in 2013) and 140th in terms of the proportion of women working or actively seeking work (44% in 2012).[122]

Women are also affected by the Church's position regarding abortion. Although it has been legal since 1984, the conditions under which abortion can be practised are very limited and it is frowned upon by the Church. And the Church's attitude to homosexuality is even more extreme. Church leaders have been reported as referring to homosexuality as a 'defect' and a 'perversion of the human existence' and a Gay Pride festival as a 'disgrace'.[123] Due in large part to Church opposition, Greece does not recognise same sex partnerships, something for which it has been criticised by the European Court of Human Rights. In a 2015 survey of support for LGBTI rights in European states, Greece ranked 21st with a score of only 39%.[124]

However, there are other traditional customs, unrelated to the Church, that also continue to be practised and in which Cretans take great pride. The most obvious examples are music and dancing. On my first visit to Crete, I remember noticing that on the coach that took us from the airport to the place where we were staying, traditional Greek music was playing. I thought this was something put on specially for tourists. It was not until sometime later, when I started to travel around the island on public buses, that I realised that it was just a local radio station. In most buses and coaches, the radio is on all the time and traditional Greek music features prominently on most radio stations. It is not the only sort of music played; modern Greek and English-language songs also feature prominently. But a significant amount of airtime is devoted to more traditional music. And it is the same on television. Several channels, especially those based in Crete, regularly broadcast traditional music programmes. Interestingly, the singers are usually men – and often middle-aged men.

Traditional Greek dancing plays an equally important part in everyday life. It is practised at festivals, weddings and other such events. Many people, both adults and children, have some knowledge of the basic steps, there are dancing classes for those who want to learn properly, and displays of traditional dancing feature prominently on television. Greek dancing is a generic form of dance, which has many regional variations. Crete, like other parts of the country, has its own specific dances, including some common to the island as a whole and others originating from particular localities.

Another important example of traditional customs is food. Cretans love food. It is probably as common a topic of conversation as the weather is in the UK! However, their tastes are much less cosmopolitan than those of many western peoples. There are very few international restaurants and, although fast food is becoming increasingly common, it has a local flavour. Cretan food, like its dancing, is similar to that in Greece as a whole, but has its own distinctive character. The island has its own particular style of cooking, featuring local produce and local recipes. It also has its own traditional drink – *raki*, which is similar to *ouzo*, but made with grain rather than grapes.

Raki originates from Turkey, and is thus a good example of the way in which Crete's history has influenced its culture. The Turkish influence on food and drink is actually much wider than one might think, not just in Crete but in Greece as a whole. Many Greek dishes and also the staple drink, coffee, originate from Turkey. 'Greek coffee' and 'Turkish coffee' are actually made in the same way, but of course one would never ask for a Turkish coffee in Greece - or vice versa. However, whatever its origins, Cretans are proud of their cuisine – and justifiably so, because it is not only delicious, but also reputed to be the healthiest in the world.

Traditional norms are also reflected in the importance attached to family life. Extended families are important (in everyday life as well as in politics) and large family parties common; older people are respected and play an important part in family life; and children are highly valued, sometimes to the point of being spoiled. As with other aspects of culture, this is slowly changing, particularly in urban areas, but the contrast with many other western nations is still evident. Moreover, it is one of the factors that has helped people to survive in times of economic downturn. During the recent recession, many unemployed young people were forced to return to live with their parents and, as I mentioned earlier, some urban residents returned to their families in the rural areas.

There is also a wider sense of community spirit and belonging, particularly but not only in rural areas. This is reflected not just in cultural activities, like village festivals, but also in a sense of trust and a relative lack of crime. For example, in the street cafés, the bill is left in a small container on the table and the customer puts the money in before he or she leaves. Similarly, shopkeepers often leave their wares outside when they close for the afternoon break (many shops and offices close around 2 pm and re-open in the evening), and cars and bicycles are often left unlocked.

And finally, no discussion of Cretan culture would be complete without mentioning the Cretan approach to time-keeping. In Crete things seldom happen at the stated time. This applies not only to private arrangements, such as social or business appointments, but also to public events, like concerts or meetings. The exception is the bus service, which, somewhat surprisingly, almost always operates on time. Both 'outsiders' and Cretans joke about Cretan time-keeping; they refer to 'Cretan time'. But Crete is not alone in this respect. In other places where I have lived and worked, there have been jokes about 'African time' and 'Melanesian time', both of which are far less reliable than 'Cretan time'. Moreover, this approach to time-keeping is part of the generally more relaxed mode of life that makes Crete an enjoyable place both to visit and to live.

Political identity

Although Crete is now an integral part of Greece, there is still a strong sense of Cretan identity and a pride in being Cretan. This is somewhat surprising, partly because of the constant movement of people between Crete and the mainland but also because the island has no special political status. As I explained in Chapter 4, the administrative region of Crete was only created in 2011 and has few meaningful powers. Moreover, there is considerable social and political fragmentation within the island, due partly to local cultural variations but also to the role of the prefectures (now known as regional units), which were the main political and administrative units for many years and continue to be the parliamentary constituencies.

As so often in such situations, people have multiple identities. They regard themselves as Greeks, but also as Cretans, and many also identify with a particular part of the island. As a Cretan friend with whom I discussed this issue said, it depends on the context. In 1965, Llewellyn Smith maintained that 'Cretans, I am sure from meeting them in all sorts of places, love their island even more than other Greeks love their own particular place'.[125] I do not know enough about other parts of Greece to judge whether this is still the case, but I suspect that it may well be so.

This sense of Cretan identity is also evident among non-Cretans, both within Greece and internationally. Mainland Greeks have always regarded Crete as somewhat different. This is reflected in the quotation from *Zorba the Greek* earlier in the chapter and in the way in which my Greek friend, Marina, reflected on her visit. And internationally, its separate identity is obvious in the tourist industry. Crete is marketed as a destination in its own right, rather than as part of Greece. I suspect that this is the main reason why the decline in tourism during the recession was not as great in Crete as in other parts of the country. Its distance from Athens, where the risk of politically motivated violence discouraged many tourists, was probably a contributing factor, but not the main one. I am sure that many tourists don't even know that Crete is part of Greece.

There are probably several reasons for this sense of separate identity. They include the semi-autonomous status of the Church of Crete and the cultural differences noted above, and also the fact that Crete has its own television and radio channels and its own newspapers. And in the case of tourism, it is possible that Crete is sometimes confused with Cyprus, which is another popular Greek-speaking tourist destination – and also begins with a 'C'! However, the main reason, and the one underlying most of the other factors, is its history. Crete has its own history and, although its history has often coincided with that of the rest of the country, this has not always been the case.

Resistance

> It was common knowledge that each Cretan kept
> a rifle at home. It was an old Cretan tradition. The
> Cretans revolted, each time the conquerors imposed
> impossible measures. This reflected the prospect of
> relative freedom that slaves occasionally impose on
> their masters. A tradition very much alive today. (Greek
> Minister of Interior, 1940; cited in George Panagiotakis,
> *The Epic Battle of Crete,* Iraklio, 2012)

> The island that has always refused to be subjugated.
> (Alexis Tsipras, Iraklio, 23 January 2015)

These two quotations reflect the image that Greeks have of Crete. The first was a comment regarding Cretans' role in the Battle of Crete in the Second World War, and the second part of Alexis Tsipras' speech in his last campaign rally prior to the 2015 elections, which was held in Iraklio. Tsipras' comment was a clever political tactic, because it implied that Cretans would want to vote for SYRIZA in order to end the subjugation of the Troika. But it was also significant in that it reflected the island's long-standing reputation for resisting exploitation.

This resistance is the third characteristic of the Cretan response to previous invasions noted in Chapter 3, and there is evidence of a similar response to the current invasion. Although Cretans seem to have decided that the benefits of this invasion have, at least so far, outweighed the costs, there have been aspects of it that they have not liked and, as in the past, they have found ways of resisting these. This resistance has taken two main forms: active and passive.

Active resistance

Any proposed government action that would affect some people adversely has been met by protests from those affected. These protests take various forms, including strikes, sit-ins, street demonstrations and online campaigns. The most obvious examples are those against the various austerity measures introduced as part of the bail-out agreement. In Greece as a whole, the period between 2010 and 2014 was marked by constant protests: strikes by civil servants against public sector cuts and reforms; strikes by private sector workers about changes in labour laws; a sit-in by staff of the state broadcasting commission in protest at its arbitrary closure; street demonstrations by those affected by the cutbacks in public services; and clashes between police and civilians over violations of human rights. And when the SYRIZA government came to power, there were also demonstrations in support of the government in its battle with the EU. The most significant of these were on 15 February 2015, when Greeks were joined by demonstrators throughout Europe.

In Crete, support for many of the national demonstrations during the austerity period was limited in extent. For example, if there was a public sector strike, local public services were not always affected, and if there was a general strike, the buses continued to run. However, protests against austerity measures with a direct local impact, such as the closure of a local health facility or changes in the local administration of the social insurance system, were strongly supported. Moreover, when it came to the 2015 elections, Cretans fulfilled Tsipras's expectations and expressed their dissatisfaction clearly. As we have already seen, SYRIZA polled 45% of the island's votes. This was significantly higher than the 36% in the country as a whole. It was the leading party in all four of the island's constituencies and in Iraklio support for SYRIZA was higher than in all but one other constituency in the country. And on 15 February 2015 there were demonstrations in support of the government in all the main towns, including one in Aghios Nikolaos that I attended.

There have also been protests about other issues of local concern. For example, during the Cold War there were demonstrations against the US/NATO military bases and, more recently, there was a major outcry in 2014 about the decontamination of nuclear weapons from Syria off the shores of western Crete.

Passive resistance

Passive resistance takes the form of non-compliance with rules and regulations. This is a more subtle form of resistance than strikes or demonstrations, and one often deeply embedded in social and political culture. It is a common phenomenon throughout Greece, but particularly prevalent in Crete.

One of the most obvious examples, and one that has a serious negative effect on the economy, is tax evasion. Greeks have long been renowned for their proficiency in avoiding paying taxes. They blame it on the Turks. The rates of taxation during the Turkish era, they say, were so high that they had to find ways of evading them.[126] However, it is also the product of a clientelistic society – a society where, if you know the right person or have the right political connections, you can get away with a great deal. Forms of tax evasion vary greatly in nature and scale. One of the most prevalent is failure to issue receipts. It is a common phenomenon among professionals, and one that I have experienced often. I have also been given receipts for less than the actual amount paid.

The reforms imposed by the Troika included various measures designed to address tax evasion. One of these was the deployment of tax collectors to tour the country, doing spot-checks on businesses. They even attended large public events, such as concerts, to make sure that revenue was properly recorded. In the first six months of 2014, they inspected 2,639 businesses, 54% of which were found to be engaged in some form of tax evasion.[127] However, this was a one-off effort and one that only caught the relatively small tax offenders. The only way of effectively addressing the problem is to change people's attitudes and, in particular, to break the pernicious link between politicians and business people. It is a problem that the SYRIZA government has recognised and pledged to tackle as its main way of improving the country's financial position. But it will not be easy because it is deeply entrenched in the social and political culture.

Another example of disregard for rules and regulations, and one that the government also tried to address during the economic crisis, relates to planning and building regulations. It was estimated in 2011 that 25% of properties in Greece violated some aspect of these regulations. The violations ranged from minor infringements, such as building extensions without planning permission or exceeding height restrictions, to the construction of entire developments without the necessary building permits or in areas not zoned for such development. In order to tackle this problem, and also raise some much needed revenue, the government introduced a law (Law 4014/2011) requiring property owners to obtain a 'certificate of regularisation' before selling or transferring their properties. In order to obtain this certificate, the properties had to be inspected by a registered professional (an architect or civil engineer) and, if any 'irregularities' were found, they had to pay a fine. Payment of this fine did not actually legalise the properties; it merely 'regularised' them for a 30-year period. The Law was introduced in September 2011 and property owners were required to regularise their properties by 31 December 2011. Regularisation after this date would be possible, but the fines would be backdated and thus higher.

I was a victim of this law. When I put my apartment up for sale because of my husband's ill health, I discovered that what I had bought as a ground floor dwelling was actually registered as a basement storage facility. Apparently, in the area where I live, which is outside the original town boundaries, one is not allowed to construct a building more than two and a half storeys high, which in effect means two storeys and a semi-basement. However, the owner of my building, like many others in the area, had ignored this regulation. He had excavated the ground deeper than indicated on the plans and, instead of a semi-basement, had built four ground floor apartments – from which he had no doubt earned considerable revenue over the years. I had to pay nearly 4,000 euros (half in fines to the government and the other half in fees to the architect who did the survey and submitted my application) to rectify the situation.

However, the impact of the law, like that of the attempts to curtail tax evasion, was very limited. Most people either could not afford to pay the fines or had 'connections' that enabled them to get around the problem. The main effects were to put the final nail in the coffin of an already collapsed property market and more money in the hands of architects and surveyors, who are already relatively well-off. And if the comments from my own architect are anything to go by, it was such a bureaucratic nightmare that some of these professionals regretted ever getting involved. The government was forced to postpone the deadline for the submission of applications for regularisation several times and eventually to amend the law to make the process both cheaper and easier.

There are many other examples of disregard for the rule of law that are less serious but more immediately obvious. One is driving habits. Cretan drivers do not have a great deal of respect for the rules of the road. They are relatively unconcerned about exceeding speed limits, jumping red lights, and double or even treble parking. Driving through Cretan towns is a slow and often hazardous process, since the streets are very narrow and one has to manoeuver one's way around the many illegally parked cars. This creates particular problems for buses, which are big and have difficulty getting through the narrow streets at the best of times. The bus drivers frequently have to stop and sound their horns to attract the attention of the driver of an illegally (or sometimes just badly) parked car that is blocking their way.

Walking through towns can also be hazardous, because in Crete, pavements are not just places for people to walk; they are also places to put the tables for your café, display various other wares, put the communal rubbish bins, park your car or motor cycle (and even abandon one you no longer want), or chain the vicious-looking dog that is guarding your property. Consequently, it is often necessary, and sometimes safer, to walk in the road. In Aghios Nikolaos a great deal of money has recently been spent on upgrading the pavements. The new pavements look very nice, but they have had little or no effect on the way in which they are used. And it is the same with pedestrian crossings. There are many such crossings and they are regularly repainted, but using them can be hazardous because one cannot assume that drivers will stop.

Another common traffic infringement relates to the wearing of helmets on motor cycles. In Greece, as elsewhere in Europe, motor cycle riders are required by law to wear a helmet. However, in Crete one frequently sees passengers without helmets, including young children - and dogs, but presumably they are not required to wear helmets. Moreover, although most drivers do wear a helmet, they are often not properly fastened. On several occasions, I have seen a motor cyclist have to stop because his or her helmet has blown off.

And finally, there is the case of smoking. As in other European countries, smoking in public places is banned in Greece. However, the Cretans are heavy smokers and the law is not strictly enforced. In cafés, there are no specially designated outside smoking areas; it is assumed that one can smoke anywhere outside – an assumption that is reinforced by the provision of ash trays. And in winter, many people also smoke inside the cafes. The resistance to comply is understandable, because the ban affects not only the customers but also the café owners, who would lose a lot of business if it were strictly enforced. One needs only to look at the fate of many of Britain's pubs to see what would happen.

Conclusion

Outsiders are often confused and sometimes also frustrated by what appear to be major contradictions in Cretans' response to their present situation. They are highly dependent on tourism, and yet one could argue that they do not do as much as they could to promote it. For example, they could do more to extend the tourist season, improve the quality of sanitary facilities, and in some respects (such as the attitude of staff in some public services) make the tourist feel more welcome. They are also dependent on foreign investment, including the purchase of property by retired immigrants like myself, and yet there are major linguistic and bureaucratic hurdles to such investment. Similarly, Cretans conform rigidly to some norms and practices, particularly those associated with religion and traditional culture, but do not hesitate to rebel against others, including many government laws and regulations. And despite their fierce independence and pride in their Cretan identity, they seem content to remain part of Greece.

However, when one remembers the island's history, these apparent contradictions begin to make sense. Cretans are responding to the present invasion in much the same way as they did to the many previous ones. They exploit the various opportunities that the invasion presents, but only as far as it is in their interests to do so and in a way that does not threaten their identity and way of life. Over the centuries, they have learned how to benefit economically from a situation without bending over backwards or losing their dignity and self-esteem. They have also learned that in order to achieve these objectives they have to be selective in their acceptance of externally imposed customs and regulations. And they have learned when to resist such impositions and how to do so.

This capacity both to exploit and to resist, to adapt and to preserve, exists to some extent in all societies. However, I would argue that it is particularly prominent in Crete and that this is because the island has been invaded so many times and by so many different peoples. This does not excuse the less attractive aspects of Cretan behaviour, such as tax evasion and dangerous driving, or reduce their negative impacts. However, it does help to explain them. Moreover, one cannot help admiring the people's resilience - and even their rebellious streak.

Chapter 6

Implications for Outsiders: We are All Guests

ξένος: foreigner, stranger; guest (*Pocket Oxford Greek Dictionary*)

The previous chapter described the ways in which Cretans have responded to the latest invasion. In this chapter, we look at the other side of the story: the implications for outsiders. We saw in Chapter 3 that in the past outsiders found it difficult to penetrate and thus control the whole island and to integrate fully into Cretan society. I will argue that it is the same today. There are a number of physical and social barriers that limit penetration and integration and enable the Cretan people to maintain the upper hand. As in the past, integration does occur, but it is not easy.

Today there are five main barriers: the physical environment, language, religion and culture, bureaucracy, and the attitudes and behaviour of the outsiders themselves. I will discuss each of these in turn. In each case, I will look both at the ways in which they limit penetration and integration and at what can be done to overcome them. In so doing, I hope also to give some idea of what life is like for an outsider in Crete.

Physical Barriers

> High mountains are revered as a place of solitude and, on occasions, the last stronghold of the eagles of

177

freedom. Although the average Cretan never sets foot in them, it is the sight of the mountains that has brought courage in the dark days of the past. (Rackham, O. and J. Moody, *The Making of the Cretan Landscape*, Manchester University Press, 1996, p.193)

Crete is a relatively small island and it is long and narrow. One might therefore think that it would be relatively easy for invaders to reach, and thus control, every part of it. However, this has never been the case in the past and, I will argue, it is not the case today. There are three main physical barriers: terrain, climate and external communications.

Terrain

As the above quotation suggests, the main physical barrier is the rugged terrain. We saw in Chapter 2 that a large part of the island is mountainous and that, although there are many lovely beaches, much of the coastline is rugged and there are relatively few natural harbours. It is a beautiful landscape, but also a harsh one.

In the past, this had two main effects. Firstly, the invaders had to struggle to penetrate many parts of the island and seldom reached the more remote areas. Consequently, as we saw in Chapter 3, most of the invasions were long, slow processes, and in many cases parts of the island were never completely controlled. Secondly, the local inhabitants were able to flee into the more inaccessible areas, where they could continue to live their own lives, surviving through subsistence farming and, if or when necessary, waging a guerrilla war against the invaders. This was the case in all the invasions, from the first Mycenaean incursions, when the Minoans retreated into the interior, to the Second World War, when the Cretan resistance established bases in the mountains.

In some respects, the situation now is very different. Over the centuries, communications have gradually improved, due in part to the efforts of the various invaders, from the Venetian construction of harbours to the EU funding of a highway from one end of the island to the other. Crete now has several ports and airports and there is a network of roads that enables one to travel not just from one end of the island to the other but to the many villages in the interior. And there are also designated walking tracks, such as the E4 footpath and the route through the Samaria Gorge, that enable the more ambitious traveller to explore some of the more remote areas.

However, the terrain still limits the extent to which the current invaders penetrate the island. For example, although there are roads up into the mountains, they are narrow, steep and winding. They are not the sort of road that many drivers would wish to tackle, particularly if, as is the case with tourists, they are driving a rented car and are not used to local driving conditions. And if one does not have a car, travel is even more restricted. The bus service is efficient, but only as a means of travel between or within major towns. And on foot the rugged terrain makes it difficult to go off the beaten track, not only inland but also along the many rugged stretches of coastline.

Consequently, as we saw in Chapter 4, most tourists only see a relatively small part of the island. Some do not venture beyond the main beaches and town centres. Others travel further afield; they visit various historical sights and beauty spots and get a taste of rural life in villages like Kritsa and Myrtos. However, they tend to keep to the main routes and so only see the more accessible places.

Many long-term residents do not do much better. Take my case. Although I do not have a car, I like to explore and see new places and so, with the help of the bus company KTEL and my own two feet, I have managed to get about quite a lot. I have visited most of the main towns on the island and, closer to home, have found many enjoyable walks, both coastal and inland. I have also been on many interesting trips with visiting friends who have hired a car, including two that gave me some idea of what life is like in the more remote parts.

One of these excursions was to the Nissimou Plateau, a small mountain plain north of the Lasithi Plateau and linked to it by an unpaved road. It is topographically similar to the Lasithi Plateau but because it is higher and more remote there is no permanent settlement. The only signs of life were an old enamel bath used as a water trough and the distant sound of goat bells, both of which indicated that it is used as a summer pasture.

The other excursion was to a remote part of the south coast, south-west of the ancient city of Gortyn. Centuries ago it was the site of a port that served Gortyn and more recently it appears to have been a small but well-patronised holiday resort, with several hotels and some upmarket Greek-owned holiday homes. But when my friends and I visited the area in June 2015 it was almost deserted. The hotel in which we stayed was the only one still open and it was about to close (that was the one bad hotel experience I mentioned in Chapter 5) and none of the holiday homes were occupied. The few people still living there appeared to have resorted to a semi-subsistence mode of life. The roads in the area were also in poor condition, having been badly damaged by rain the previous winter and only partially repaired. It was not clear why the area had declined; we suspected that the main reason was the recession but that the damage caused by the weather had been the final straw. It gave us some idea of what life might be like in Crete if, for any reason, there was a major economic collapse.

However, these were merely glimpses. I still feel that I have an incomplete picture of the island. Moreover, even in my own neighbourhood there are many places that I have failed to access. The most obvious example is Thilakas, the hill that rises five hundred metres above my house. One of my ambitions has always been to climb it, but it is one I have yet to achieve. In this and many other cases, the barrier is not just the terrain but the vegetation. As I explained in Chapter 2, much of Crete is covered by *maquis*, a sort of scrubland comprising a dense mass of stunted trees, shrubs and herbaceous plants, many of them prickly. The only way of penetrating this (other than by setting out armed with a *machete*) is to follow a goat path. However, these paths tend to peter out after a while - and goats can go in places where humans cannot, such as over rocky inclines or under low branches. Every time I venture on an excursion through *maquis*, I come back exhausted, scratched to pieces and frustrated because I failed to get where I wanted.

There are also man-made physical barriers on these walks. The two main ones are fences and dogs. Most if not all of the land appears to belong to someone and many people have erected fences to mark their boundaries and prevent their livestock straying. People also use dogs to protect their property. As I mentioned in the previous chapter, many urban dwellers have small rural plots, where they keep a few goats, sheep and chickens, and they leave a dog to guard the premises. The dogs are usually either fenced in or chained, but one has to be careful in case they are not. And even if they cannot actually attack you, their barking is enough to discourage one from approaching. This is a problem even in built up areas, since many occupied properties have guard dogs, especially if the owners are away during the day. Walking along such roads is like walking through a dog kennels; the first dog one passes starts barking, and then the next takes up the call, and so it goes on.

It is possible for outsiders to venture into more remote areas. A few tourists, like the friends with whom I visited the Nissimou Plateau and the deserted south coast resort, do venture off the beaten track. And some long-term residents make more effort than I have done to explore the interior of the island, some by vehicle and others on foot. However, it is not easy. For the majority of expatriates, the more practical solution is to follow the example of today's Cretans and merely enjoy the mountains from a distance. As the quotation at the beginning of this section implies, most Cretans now live either in towns or in villages that are relatively accessible; it is only the shepherds who venture into the more remote areas. However, there is an important difference between Cretans and outsiders in that, as the quotation suggests, the Cretans value the mountains not just for their beauty but also as a refuge. The mountains remind them of their history and the knowledge that they are there should the need arise again provides a sense of security.

Climate

Climate is another major physical barrier. This may at first sight seem odd, since Crete's climate is one of the island's main attractions, particularly for tourists and long-term residents. However, as we saw in Chapter 2, the climate is far more varied than one might expect.

Most tourists do not experience the full range of climatic conditions. Most guidebooks suggest that the best time to visit Crete is either between April and June or in September or October. They warn that July and August can be unpleasantly hot, while in the winter months it can be cold and wet. The length of the tourist season is gradually increasing and, as I mentioned in the previous chapter, some people believe that winter tourism should be promoted. However, I have some reservations about this, not only because it could disturb Cretans' winter lives, but also because a winter holiday could be very risky. At that time of the year it can sometimes rain heavily for two or three days at a time and, if one is only visiting for a week, that is a significant portion of one's holiday. When it rains heavily, there is very little that one can do, even in the towns, since the roads are often ankle deep in water, and holiday accommodation can be damp and inadequately heated.

However, even if one comes at the recommended times of year, one may get a glimpse of the other side of the Cretan climate.

For example, when my husband and I visited Crete as tourists, we came in September, not because of the guidebooks' advice but because it was the best time for me to take time off work and it was nice to have a week in the sun to 'charge up one's batteries' (as my husband put it) in preparation for the British winter. However, we seldom had a week of unbroken good weather. The first visit was marred by three days of cool, cloudy conditions and the second by three days of gale force winds, which at times were so strong that my husband dared not venture out for fear of being blown over. On the next two visits we were luckier, but it was often very windy. By the time that we made the decision to move to Crete, we had accepted the fact that, as Rackham and Moody say, 'Crete is a windy island'.[128]

For long-term residents, the vagaries of the climate are less of a problem, because one can take the rough with the smooth. Even in winter, a period of cold wet weather is inevitably followed by one or two lovely sunny days, when one can sit outside or go for long walks – and also dry one's laundry and air one's damp bedding. Many expatriates like the winter, regarding it as a break from the heat of summer. Personally, I prefer the summer; winter is something that I merely tolerate. Part of the problem is that buildings and infrastructure are often inadequately equipped for winter. For example, my apartment, like many others, is designed to keep heat out rather than in. It has no damp course, south-facing windows or central heating. And the semi-rural road on which I live has no proper drainage, so when it rains the road becomes a river and one needs wellington boots to venture outside.

However, the problems I face in winter are minor compared with those that people living at higher altitudes have to endure. As I explained in Chapter 2, on the coast, the temperature seldom drops below zero and snow is a rare phenomenon, but in the mountains it is several degrees colder and there is snow every winter. According to Rackham and Moody, the temperature drops by at least 6° for every 1000 metres.[129] One does not have to go far to notice the difference. The snow that fell in Aghios Nikoloas in January 2015 soon melted. However, the next day I went up to the nearby village of Kritsa, which is about 300 metres above sea level, and was surprised by the amount of snow still lying around. And up in the Lasithi Plateau, people were cut off for several days.

Rackham and Moody question why there is no settlement above 800 metres in Crete. They say that winters in the Lasithi Plateau, which is at this altitude, are no worse than those in the English Lake District and wonder why 'the inhabitants regard this as hardship, and leave if they possibly can'.[130] However, I do not find this surprising. I am not sure why, but for some reason or other, bad weather in Crete is worse than bad weather in the UK. One possible reason is the extremes. In summer, it is extremely hot and dry, while in winter it can rain continuously for two or three days and, even if it is not raining, everything is very damp. Moreover, when it is windy, it is incredibly windy. Apparently, it is not only elderly people like my husband who risk being blown over by the wind. Rackham and Moody report that they 'have seen stones blown away' and have themselves 'been blown over by gusts'.[131]

Moreover, as I mentioned in Chapter 2, the weather is very variable, especially in winter. It can be warm and sunny one day and cold and wet the next. Sometimes the change occurs in a matter of hours. In the summer, strong hot winds blow up out of nowhere, while in winter the day may begin warm, but then the wind changes direction or there is a violent thunder storm, often accompanied by gale force winds, and temperatures drop dramatically. The diurnal changes in temperature are also often high; a ten degree difference between the maximum and minimum temperatures is not uncommon. Crete's climate, like its terrain, can be harsh.

This harshness is well portrayed by Victoria Hislop in her novel, *The Island*, which is set on Spinalonga.[132] Although Spinalonga is on the coast, it is very exposed and, since it is rocky and barren, there is little or no shelter from either the hot sun of summer or the cold winds of winter. Hislop provides a vivid description of the hardships faced by the lepers who were banished there, especially in the early days, when they were accommodated in the dilapidated Turkish buildings.

What can one do about this? For the tourist, the answer is to follow the guidebooks' advice and come when the weather is most likely to be favourable. Most tourists do this if they can. Those with children are often forced to come in July or August, which are thus busy months. However, they tend to spend most of their time on the beach. For the long-term resident, there are two possible solutions. One is to spend part of the year elsewhere. Many retired expatriates do this; they return to their country of origin either in July and August or for part of the winter, depending on which aspects of the climate they like and dislike. The other is to do what one would do in any other part of the world: make sure that both one's house and one's wardrobe are adequately equipped for all seasons - and when the weather is inclement, grin and bear it!

External communications

Although Crete now has commercial ports and airports, as well as efficient telecommunications, it is still an island. Travel to and from it is thus restricted by unexpected events, such as stormy weather or air controllers' strikes, and more significantly, by airline and ferry schedules. In order to appreciate the extent and impact of these restrictions, and also the reasons for them, let us take a closer look at airline schedules.

I have already said something about air traffic to and from Crete in Chapter 4. There are three main features. Firstly, in summer there are numerous flights to all sorts of places, but in winter the only direct flights are to the Greek mainland. Secondly, most of the flights are operated by either tour operators or budget airlines. And thirdly, the main flight destinations in summer are western Europe and Russia. Aegean Airlines operates a summer service between Iraklio and Cyprus and in 2013 it introduced one between Iraklio and Istanbul, but there are not many flights on these routes and there are none to North Africa or other parts of the Middle East.

Why is this? There are two main reasons. One is that air schedules are dominated by the tourist industry, which (as we saw in Chapter 4) has a particular season and clientele and is based on the concept of the package holiday. The other is that Crete is part of Greece and, as in many countries, communications within Greece are centred on the capital city, which is Athens. However, the fact that Cretans have made no effort to change this pattern suggests that it may also reflect a desire, albeit perhaps unconscious, to limit the nature and extent of their relations with the outside world – and particularly with the non-Greek speaking world. The introduction of a service to Istanbul suggests that this may be changing. But in the meantime, long-term residents, like Cretans, have to travel either on the seasonal flights designed for tourists or via Athens.

The Language Barrier

> The limits of my tongue are my boundaries. (Greek proverb)[133]

In the previous chapter, I noted that, although English is widely spoken and used as a means of communication with foreigners, Greek is the language of choice for other purposes. It is the language used in everyday life, in government, in literature and in the media. In my view, this is probably the most significant barrier to integration that today's invaders face. As the above proverb says, it limits one's boundaries. It makes it difficult to participate fully in Cretan society, let alone comprehend it, and it makes the outsider vulnerable not only to misunderstanding but also to exploitation. I will use three examples from my own experience to illustrate this point.

The first example is that of everyday conversation. Although many Cretans speak reasonable English, there are relatively few who are able to take part in an in-depth discussion about issues such as history, literature or politics. I am particularly interested in politics and in the run-up to both the 2014 European elections and the 2015 national elections, I longed for the opportunity to have a serious discussion with local people about the issues at stake and their own personal views. I did my best to follow the campaigns. For example, in 2014 I went to Ierapetra to hear Alexis Tsipras, SYRIZA's leader, speak. I could not follow much of what he said, but it was an interesting experience. And prior to the 2015 elections I helped INCO, a local expatriate organisation which I will say more about later, organise meetings for its members with local representatives of some of the parties. The meeting with the SYRIZA representatives was particularly interesting and gave me some sort of insider view. However, with a better knowledge of Greek, I could have learned much more.

The second example is bureaucracy. I will say more about this later, but the point I wish to make here is that all documentation is in Greek, and only in Greek. This makes life for expatriate residents difficult. All the documents related to day-to-life, from the contract one signs when purchasing a property to tax returns and service bills are in Greek. Moreover, if for any reason one has to submit an English document, such as a birth or marriage certificate, one is often required to have it translated into Greek. Therefore, if one doesn't speak the language, one is dependent on intermediaries, such as estate agents, lawyers and accountants, to handle one's business.

The third example is the media. As I mentioned in Chapter 5, neither in Crete nor in Greece as a whole, is there any English language daily newspaper or any radio or television station that broadcasts a news bulletin in English. Fortunately, there are some good online sources that provide regular news reports. I rely on two main ones: *ekathimerini.com,* which is the English version of an online Greek newspaper, and *Greek Reporter*.[134] I find that reading these online English sources helps me to follow the news in Greek on television, which I watch every evening, partly to follow events but also to practise my Greek.

The answer to these problems is, of course, to learn Greek. Anyone who chooses to live in a foreign country should expect to have to learn the language. However, in Crete very few outsiders have a good working knowledge of Greek. The English are probably the worst offenders. This is not surprising, partly because one can get by in English but also because we are notoriously bad at learning other languages. A notable exception apparently is Victoria Hislop. In 2014 she was awarded the freedom of the town of Aghios Nikolaos and I am told that she gave her speech of thanks in Greek. Other nationalities tend to do better, especially the unskilled economic migrants who have to speak Greek in order to get work. However, although these migrants speak the language reasonably well, their vocabulary and grammatical skills tend to be limited and they are often unable to write in Greek.

Many people, like me, make an effort to learn the language. In 2008, the Greek government, with funding from the EU, launched a programme, known as *Odysseus*, for the teaching of Greek to immigrants. The programme is intended primarily for economic migrants, but the lessons, which are free, are open to anyone. The programme is organised on a regional basis and, thanks to the efforts of a dynamic regional organiser, there are courses throughout the Lasithi region where I live, which includes the three municipalities of Aghios Nikolaos, Ierapetra and Sitia. In 2013-14, there were 21 courses in the region, running concurrently and each with between ten and fifteen students. There were two in Sitia, five in Aghios Nikolaos and fourteen in Ierapetra. The large number in Ierapetra can be explained by the many economic migrants working on the farms in the area.[135] The courses, which are run in winter, last four or five months, with sessions held two or three times a week. I have attended two such courses.

I have also, as I mentioned in Chapter 4, attended two intensive one-month courses designed primarily for Russian students. They were organised by the local Church, as part of a move to strengthen relationships between the Greek and Russian Orthodox Churches, and most of the students had some connection with the Church. Attending these courses was an interesting experience, in which I not only improved my Greek but also learned a considerable amount about the nature and role of the Orthodox Church in both countries.

The formal courses focus mainly on grammar and written work. After a while, I found that I had acquired a reasonable knowledge of grammar and could write better than many students, but I was unable to carry on a simple conversation. In 2014 I therefore decided to supplement these efforts with weekly lessons from a private teacher. These lessons are held in groups of four or five students and, although there is some grammar and written work, the focus is on conversation – and the teacher is excellent. These are the most useful classes I have attended.

However, despite all these efforts, my knowledge of the language remains frustratingly limited and, as I indicated above, this in turn limits my ability to participate effectively in everyday life. My lack of progress is due primarily to my own deficiencies. I have never been a good linguist, especially when it comes to actually speaking a language, and my age does not help; the saying that 'one cannot teach an old dog new tricks' is particularly applicable when it comes to languages. Furthermore, like many expatriates, I do not make enough effort to use Greek. In my case, the problem is not so much that I socialise with other expatriates (an issue to which I will return later in the chapter), but that I spend a lot of time on my own, writing and reading in English.

However, it is generally recognised that Greek is not an easy language to learn and I am not the only person who has problems. I was both surprised and reassured to learn that a Slovenian friend, who speaks seven different languages (including fluent

English) and has spent much of the last ten years in Greece, finds Greek exceptionally hard. I was also interested to read in a book by John Humphrys, the renowned British journalist and radio and television broadcaster, that his son Christopher, who is married to a Greek and has lived in the country for many years, still struggles with the language. I will say more about this book, which is called *Blue Skies and Black Olives*,[136] later in the chapter.

There are several reasons why Greek is difficult to learn. Some of these relate to the language itself. The most obvious one is the alphabet. This is not a problem in conversation, but it is a significant obstacle when it comes to reading and writing. Another problem is the grammar, especially the many different forms that words take. Nouns and pronouns vary, depending on the number (singular or plural), gender (masculine, feminine or neutral) and case (nominative, accusative, genitive, or vocative); adjectives have to match the noun and so also vary; and verbs vary in form, depending on the person and tense, much more than they do in English. In this respect, Greek is very like Latin, and more like French or German than English.

However, there are also problems due to the way in which the language is used. Firstly, Greeks tend to speak very fast. This makes it difficult for someone with only a rudimentary knowledge of the language to follow what is being said. And secondly, they tend to speak and, in particular, write in a somewhat long-winded manner. I have sat for hours with a dictionary trying to translate things like electricity bills or the instructions for a new appliance, only to find out that the information is actually very simple. The combination of speaking quickly and writing at length has an interesting effect when it comes to translation. If an English speech is translated into Greek orally (for example, when dubbed in a film or television interview), the Greek version will take less time than the English. But if the same speech is in written form, the Greek version is significantly longer.

However, despite these problems, some outsiders do become

fluent in Greek and the benefits are evident: they are able to participate in the local society much more than those who do not. There are two main groups. The first are adults who have lived and often also worked on the island for many years and, in many cases, are married to Greeks. The second are the children of expatriates, who have to speak Greek at school and, like children everywhere, learn very quickly. However, there are a few others, such as Alex, the Cyprus-born Englishman whom I mentioned in Chapter 4.

Moreover, although Greek is a difficult language to learn, the process of trying to learn it is in itself a worthwhile experience. For an English-speaker, it is a fascinating language because of the way in which it has influenced English. Some of these influences are very obvious and well known. For example, in science and medicine, many English words are derived directly from the Greek. However, others are less obvious and can even be confusing. The Greek alphabet illustrates this. For example, the Greek letter β looks like and is obviously the origin of the English letter *b*. However, it is pronounced like a *v*; the sound *b* is written by combining the letters μ (which is pronounced *m*) and π (pronounced *p*). The Greek letter ν is equally confusing; although written like a *v*, it is actually an *n*; the capital form, N, is the same as in English. Another example is the word δύo, meaning *two*, which is obviously the origin of the English prefix *duo*. However, in Greek the letter δ is pronounced *th* (as in *the*, not as in *third*) and the letter υ is pronounced *i* (as in *it*); so the word δύo is pronounced *the-o*.

This can cause problems when it comes to writing Greek names in English - for example, the names of places on maps and road signs. In Crete, for instance, there is confusion over the spelling of the main town, Ηράκλειο. In English, this is often written as *Heraklio*, but that is not strictly correct. The Greek letter H (which in the lower case is written as η), is obviously the origin of the English letter H, but it is pronounced *i*. The correct spelling is therefore *Iraklio*. In this case, the confusion is compounded by the fact that Ηράκλειο was once known as Ηράκλειον, so in English it is often written as *Heraklion*. And to confuse things even further, place names, like other nouns, vary in form, depending on their gender and the context in which they are used. For example, the town where I live is called Άγιος Νικόλαος. But that is the nominative form of its name – in other words, the form used when it is the subject of the sentence. If one wants to say, for example, that one is going *to* the town, one has to use the accusative (or object) form, which is Άγιο Νικόλαο. There is also a genitive form, but I won't confuse you further with that!

There are also some words that are confusing because they are different from the English. For example, the Greek word νότος (pronounced *notos*) means south, not north. The word for north is βορεάς (pronounced *vorias*), which is presumably where the English word *voracious* comes from. And even more confusing perhaps is the translation of the phrase *ante meridian (am)*, which is πάρα μεσημέρι. This is abbreviated to πμ, which in English script is *pm*! The Greek translation of *post meridian (pm)* is μέτα μεσημέρι, which is abbreviated as μμ, which in English is *mm*. One therefore has to be very careful when reading messages or notices that indicate the time of a meeting or event; otherwise one could turn up in the evening for an event that occurred in the morning!

And finally, to add to all this confusion, there are also differences in punctuation. In English, a semicolon (;) is used to indicate a major break in a sentence, something in between a comma and a full stop. But in Greek, it is used at the end of a sentence to indicate a question. This appears to be a carry-over from Ancient Greek. According to *Wikipedia*, something called an *interpunct* (·) is used to indicate a major break in a sentence in Greek. However, one seldom sees an *interpunct*. Greeks tend just to use either a comma or a full stop.[137]

I find these insights and puzzles intriguing. They demonstrate the complexity of the process whereby languages develop and change over time – and also the way in which information can be distorted through translation, as in the case of the confusion between juniper and cedar trees mentioned in Chapter 2. For me, they more than compensate for the frustrations of trying to learn Greek, and have encouraged me to persevere with my efforts.

Religious and Cultural Exclusion

> *Nationalism*: policy of national independence; patriotism, sometimes to an excessive degree. (*Collins English Dictionary*)

In the previous chapter, we saw that religion and traditional culture play an important role in Cretan society and that Cretans are proud of their cultural heritage. We saw also that this is one of the attractions for the visitor. The many little whitewashed churches, perched precariously on mountaintops; the delicious Cretan food, served in picturesque *tavernas*; the traditional music and dancing: these are the things that, along with the scenery and climate, bring so many people to the island.

However, there is another side to this story. In Crete, as in Greece as a whole, religion and culture, together with language, have been used to foster a sense of national identity and pride; in other words, to promote nationalism. And, as the above definition suggests, nationalism can be both positive and negative. Pride in one's culture and national identity can be beneficial, especially when trying to unify a divided people; but if carried to excess, it can lead to prejudice against other cultures, biased interpretation of events and exclusion of 'outsiders'. I was interested to learn that the Greek word for 'foreigner' is ξένος, which is pronounced *xenos* and is the origin of the English word *xenophobia*.

In Chapter 3 we saw how this nationalism has evolved over time and how it has had some negative effects, such as the exchange of Moslems and Christians in the 1920s, and how it has affected the writing of history; and, although Greece has now been independent for many years, elements remain today. One example is foreign relations, where, as we have already seen, religion continues to play a major role, fostering positive ties with Russia and hampering relations with Turkey. Another example is the role of traditional culture in the education system. In May 2015, I happened to read that students sitting one of the Greek university entrance examinations that were then taking place were required to write a speech for a municipal meeting on why Greeks must protect and promote their cultural heritage. What most interested me was not this fact in itself but the reaction of the Greek reporter, who questioned how long Greeks should continue to 'invoke that legacy as an alibi or as proof of our racial superiority'.[138]

In Crete, now as in the past, this religious and cultural pride can be a barrier for outsiders. It is easy for an outsider to observe and enjoy traditional mores and customs, but much more difficult to become an active participant, and in particular to be accepted as such. In order to illustrate this point, I will look at three examples of situations where outsiders have either tried or been forced by circumstances to become active participants in their local society, with varying degrees of success.

The first example is that of expatriates living in villages. As I noted in Chapter 4, many long-term residents choose to live in villages. For them, the chance to live in a renovated traditional house and participate in local village life is one of the attractions of Crete. These people obviously see a side of life that I, living in a town, do not. However, are they really able to participate fully in village life and how are they regarded by local residents? I had a discussion about this one day with two Englishmen who live in villages near Neapoli. We were with a group of expatriates in a *taverna* in the village where one of them lived. I asked this man whether he considered himself to be part of the village. He said that he did. He described how he dropped into the local καφενείο every day for a cup of coffee, often ate in the local *taverna,* and participated in local festivities. He was not fluent in Greek, but spoke enough to carry on a simple conversation. However, the other man questioned this. He reckoned, based on his own experience, that despite this man's efforts, he was merely a 'participant observer' and that, although the villagers were happy to have him there, he was not accepted as a full member of the village.

I tend to agree with the second opinion. It is very difficult for an outsider to be fully integrated into any small rural community. I am reminded once again of the anthropologists I met in Papua New Guinea (see Chapter 3), who spent years living in and studying remote rural societies but often misinterpreted what they saw. They liked to think that they were fully accepted into the local society, but they never were. It is not just the cultural differences or even the language barrier that makes integration difficult, but also the strong sense of local identity and community. And in Crete this is reinforced by the people's pride in their culture – a pride that is often tinged with a feeling of superiority.

The second example is that of expatriates who join the Greek Orthodox Church. This is not a common phenomenon. Most expatriates are non-religious or continue to practise their own religion in some way or other. However, I have come across three people who have become members of the Orthodox Church. Two of these are English and both happen to live in Elounda. One is Chris Moorey. He has not only become an active Church member but also written three books about the Orthodox Church in Crete.[139] The other is Amy (not her real name). She lives on her own and the Church plays an important role in her life. She is fully conversant with all the religious practices and customs, observes all the festivals and also takes an active part in pastoral activities.

The third person is Ezekiel. His case is very different. He is from Uganda and, when I met him, he was a student at a seminary in Iraklio. I don't know how he came to be there. Was he recruited by the Church in his home country or did he come as an economic migrant and then get involved in the Church? He was very reticent when I questioned him about his past. He was not training to be a priest but to be a religious artist, painting religious pictures, or icons as they are generally known. However, like Amy, he appeared to be totally committed to the Church.

It cannot have been easy for any of these people to join the Orthodox Church. It is not only distinctly different from other Christian churches but also, as we have seen, quite conservative and dogmatic in some of its attitudes and, once again, there is an element of superiority in its attitude to other religions. It must have been particularly difficult for Ezekiel, coming from Africa. There is very little knowledge of Africa or Africans in Crete and thus many misconceptions and a degree of prejudice. Interestingly, however, the feelings are not entirely one-sided. When I asked Ezekiel what he was going to do when he graduated, he said his first priority was to get married – but, in a rare moment of frankness, he added that he would not marry a Greek woman!

However, despite these problems, membership of the Church has enabled Chris, Amy and Ezekiel to integrate better into local society than most outsiders. It has helped Chris to understand the society in which he is living and thus to write books about it. It has helped Amy not only to find a meaning and purpose in life but also to gain a working knowledge of Greek and become part of the Elounda community. And for Ezekiel, who speaks fluent Greek, it has provided the economic and legal security that most African migrants lack.

The third example is that of women who have lived in Crete for many years and who (unlike Ezekiel) have chosen to marry Cretans. In many respects these people are not outsiders. They speak the language, follow local customs, have Greek friends and relatives, and in many cases have reared children in the local Cretan environment. However, one gets the impression that it has not always been easy. They have had not only to learn the local language and customs, but also to accept what some would regard as the somewhat subservient position of Greek women. They have had to be devoted wives and mothers and competent housekeepers – and in particular to learn to cook Greek food! Moreover, one senses that in some respects they still feel like, and are regarded as, outsiders.

One might argue that such problems occur in all inter-cultural marriages. However, the difficulties do seem to be greater than one would expect to find in a marriage between two Europeans. I suspect that this is due partly to the cultural differences but also to the Cretans pride in their culture, which means that it is the outsider who has to make most of the concessions. Another, and perhaps more valid, argument is that it is always difficult for first generation migrants. The children of such marriages integrate much more easily because they grow up as Cretans. They learn to speak Greek at an early age, attend local schools and have local friends. Even those who later go to the UK or elsewhere to study or work regard Crete as home. Their position is very different not just to that of their parents but also to that of the children of expatriates, who are apparently often bullied at school, particularly if they do not speak Greek well. In other words, as in the past, integration is possible, but it takes time and it is generally on Cretan terms.

Bureaucratic Hurdles

> Dealing with Greek officialdom is like trying to wade through a lake of treacle wearing a heavy overcoat and lead-lined boots with your eyes blindfolded.
> (John Humphrys, *Blue Skies and Black Olives*, Hodder and Stoughton, 2009)

John Humphrys' book, *Blue Skies and Black Olives*, was one of the things that inspired me to write a book about Crete. The book tells how he and his son Christopher bought a plot of land in the Peloponnese. It describes the long and tortuous process they went through to build a house on the land, and in so doing provides fascinating insights into life in Greece – and also into the relationship between John and Christopher. The book was published in 2009, but I didn't read it until March 2014. At the time, I was battling with the Greek bureaucracy in an attempt to address one of the many administrative problems associated with my apartment and I decided that, if they could write a book about their experiences, I could write one about mine. I knew that publication would be much more difficult for me than for the Humphrys because, like so many things in life, getting a book published is more about who you are and whom you know than your personal abilities. However, I decided that I would face up to that challenge when the time came. In an original draft of the book, I had a chapter called *Blue Skies, Black Olives and Red Tape* – a title that I am surprised John Humphrys did not consider!

A case study

The particular problem that I was tackling at the time related to my electricity supply. I had just found out that my little two-roomed apartment was registered as a commercial property, which meant that I was paying higher taxes and electricity charges than necessary. I learned this by accident. I was paying a bill for one of my neighbours, who was in the UK at the time, and I happened to notice that he was paying a lower rate for electricity than me. When I enquired at the local office of the Public Power Corporation, known by everyone as ΔEH (pronounced like 'they'), the receptionist referred me to a man in an upstairs office who explained the reason.

Suspecting that there was a connection between this and the fact that (as I explained in the previous chapter) the apartment had been registered as storage space, I went back to the architect who had handled the 'regularisation' and asked his advice. After making some enquiries, he told me that, in addition to proof of the regularisation, which he could provide, I would have to have an electrical survey of the property done, to ensure that it complied with current electricity regulations. He offered to recommend me to an electrician who could do the survey and, since I didn't know any qualified electricians, I accepted his offer.

The electrician came a few days later. It was a miserable winter day, cold and pouring with rain. He was not a particularly communicative man and his English was not much better than my Greek, but he was very thorough. He was there a couple of hours and checked everything, inside and outside the apartment. He said there were a lot of problems, but because of the language barrier I could not understand exactly what was wrong. He said he would send me a report. When he left, the apartment was bitterly cold, there were muddy footprints all over the floor and I had a feeling that this was going to be another long battle.

It was several weeks before the report arrived. It was translated into English, but due partly to poor translation but also to my lack of technical knowledge about electrical matters, I was not much wiser about the precise nature of the problems. What I did gather, however, was that it would cost me about 1,500 euros to have them rectified and prepare the survey report for ΔEH. The main cost, it appeared, would be to improve the 'grounding', which would involve hiring a machine and drilling a number of holes. Since one could not determine in advance the exact number of holes required, the price quoted was merely an estimate and the actual figure could be considerably more. I calculated that it would be at least five years before the benefits in terms of lower electricity charges outweighed the costs incurred in doing the work and, after some thought, decided that it was not worth it.

However, the day after I made this decision, I had an electrical problem. About 8.30 pm I switched on a light and the bulb blew. It was not the first time this had happened with this particular light. However, this time, the problem was more serious, because it blew my whole electricity supply. The 'odd job' man whom I would normally have called on for help was away and I did not want to contact the electrician who had done the survey. I therefore phoned a friend for advice. She suggested that, since I had no power whatsoever, I should contact ΔEH, the electricity company. They were wonderful! They came almost immediately. They said that the supply into the property was okay so the problem must be in my apartment, and that was not their responsibility. However, when they saw that I had no idea what to do now, they took pity on me and came inside. They found that the main fuse had blown and put in a new one.

After that event, I decided that I had better get an electrician to check the light. It so happened that a couple of days later, I had a dentist's appointment. I had got to know the dentist quite well, so I asked him if he could recommend an electrician. He gave me the name of a man who had recently done some electrical work for him. I phoned this man and he came the next day. He was very nice and, unlike the previous one, spoke good English. He concluded that the problem with the light was simply that I was using the wrong type of bulb. However, he also pointed out that I did not have what he called a 'relay'. I didn't know what a 'relay' was, but I did know that it was one of the things that the other electrician had said that I needed. It was not until sometime later, when the 'relay' was fitted, that I realised it is what in the UK is called a circuit breaker.

When the second electrician mentioned that I needed a 'relay', I told him about the earlier survey. He took one look at the report and said that it was ridiculous. The only things that I needed were the circuit breaker and one new socket. He said that the 'grounding' work was not necessary and that, if it were done, it would benefit the whole building, so the costs should be shared between all the occupants. He said he could do everything that needed to be done and prepare the report for ΔEH for about 400 euros. Needless to say, I was overjoyed.

A few days later, he phoned me to say that he had all the papers ready for me and offered to bring them round immediately so that I could take them to ΔEH. When I looked at the papers, I found that they included a receipt for the work done. When I pointed out that he had not yet done the work and I had not paid him, he said that was no problem; he would do it the following day and I could pay him then. I decided that this was perhaps a good idea, because if I encountered a problem at ΔEH, he would have to sort it out before I paid him. I also noticed that the papers included an electrical plan of the apartment. I wondered how he had prepared that since, unlike the previous electrician, he had not done a detailed survey. But I decided not to ask any questions.

I had assumed that all I had to do now was take the papers to ΔEH, and that would be that. However, needless to say, it was not so simple. I went to see the man in the upstairs office at ΔEH, who checked them and said they were okay. But he told me that now I had to pay a 60 euro fee to the Association of Electrical Workers, otherwise known as ΣHE (pronounced 'See'). In order to do this, I had to go to a particular bank and pay the money into ΣHE's account. This is a common practice in Greece, presumably intended to reduce the risk of corruption. I then took the receipt of payment to the ΣHE office, where a lady checked the papers and then put an official stamp on each of the four pages. She then told me to go to a stationery shop round the corner and make three photocopies. I returned to ΣHE, left a copy with the lady there, and then made my way back to ΔEH.

Back in the upstairs office at ΔEH, the man said that was fine, but now he needed to see my passport. I cursed myself; one needs one's passport for so many transactions in Greece that I should have thought to bring it with me. He was sympathetic. He said that they probably already had a copy on their files and could use that; but when he found it, I remembered that I now had a new passport, so the copy he had was no longer valid. Once again he was sympathetic. He said I could bring a copy of the new passport in later. He then gave me some papers and told me to take them to the office downstairs. When I got there, the lady at the desk asked to see my passport. I told her that it had been agreed that I would bring it in later, but she insisted that she must see it. And she also said that she needed a copy of the contract for my apartment and a meter reading. Unlike the man upstairs, she was not the sort of person one could try to reason with.

It was a Friday and I wanted to get the task finished that day. I therefore went home (the ΔEH office is about 20 minutes' walk from my apartment), collected the required documents and read the meter, and then returned to the office. The lady was satisfied. She then gave me another piece of paper and told me to take this to the cashier and pay a 30 euro connection fee. By now it had dawned on me that I was not simply changing the status of my property; I was opening a totally new electricity account. The queue at the cashier's was quite long and, while waiting, I decided that I had better find out whether the direct debit arrangement that I had with my bank would still be valid. When I returned to the other office with the receipt for the connection fee, I asked the lady and was not surprised when she told me that I would have to set up a new direct debit. I sighed. Like everything else in Greece, setting up a direct debit is not easy. The original one consisted of a ten page contract between myself and the bank, each page of which I had to initial. My bank had since been taken over by a larger one, so maybe the process would be simpler now. However, I decided not to find out. I would do what most Greeks still do and go into the ΔEH office to pay my bills.

The following day, the electrician came as promised. He put in the circuit breaker and changed the socket, and I paid him the money. I was very happy. The whole process had taken only a week and the total cost, including the fee to ΣHE and the connection charge, was only 460 euros. And that included VAT, which for all but essential items was then 23%.

What exactly is the problem?

My experience is not unusual. It is widely acknowledged, by

Greeks as well as outsiders, that Greek bureaucracy is a nightmare. One of my Greek text books, intended primarily for economic migrants, includes a whole chapter designed to help students find their way through the bureaucratic maze. The chapter is called 'In the Queue'!

I have described the above example at some length, because it illustrates not only the nature of the problem but also the causes. As the case study suggests, there are several causal factors. One is the complexity of the bureaucratic system, much of which dates back to the period of Turkish rule and some even further. Another is the power of the professions, including lawyers, accountants, architects, electricians, doctors and dentists, which is protected by law. A third factor is the role of patronage, which means that the most effective way of getting something done is to know the right person. And, last but not least, there is the problem of lack of respect for the rule of law, which I discussed in detail in Chapter 5.

These factors are all interrelated and deeply entrenched in the Greek political culture. For example, professionals are powerful not just because they are protected by the law but also because the bureaucracy is so complex that ordinary citizens cannot operate the system on their own. According to my accountant, very few people in Greece submit their own tax returns; they all have an accountant who does it for them. The recent introduction of online tax returns has not changed the situation much, because the systems are geared for use by accountants rather than ordinary people; moreover, in Crete there are still many people who do not use the internet. The power of professionals in turn fuels the patronage system, because they operate by cultivating contacts in the corridors of power. And disregard for the rule of law, although blamed on Turkish occupation, is really a product of all the other three. Moreover, as we saw in Chapter 5, it is something in which Greeks in general, and Cretans in particular, actually take pride.

And for the outsider, of course, there is the additional problem of language. Expatriates, as I have already mentioned, have no choice but to operate through professional intermediaries, such as lawyers and accountants, and this makes them particularly vulnerable. Even if one has a reasonable knowledge of Greek, one needs such people because of the complexity of the language used in official documents. Many of the problems I have encountered in relation to my apartment stem from my inability to read such documents - and of course my negligence in not getting them translated.

Wider implications

The nightmare of Greek bureaucracy does not only affect individuals like me. It was also a major obstacle to the implementation of the reforms imposed upon Greece by the Troika between 2010 and 2014. For example, attempts to reduce the size of the public service were hampered by politicians' reluctance to lose one of their main means of patronage, moves to introduce new forms of taxation were a shambles owing to the complexity of public service procedures and politicians' attempts to thwart the changes, and progress in privatising state services and assets was fraught by corruption and political resistance.

For me, this came as no surprise, because I had seen the same thing in Africa. The 'structural adjustment' reforms imposed on many African countries in the 1980s and '90s were severely hampered by problems such as patronage, corruption and an inefficient bureaucracy. I mentioned in Chapter 4 that students of development studies learned long ago that these reforms tend to create more problems than they solve. They also learned that it is very difficult to introduce such reforms in countries with deep-seated political and administrative weaknesses. One has to first address the underlying problems, and this is something that can only be done from the inside.

What did surprise (and also anger) me was that no-one seemed to have learned anything from the African experience. Two factors made this particularly frustrating. One was that the IMF was a party to both sets of reforms, so should have learned from its own experience. The other was the Troika's attitude to SYRIZA, both in the run-up to the 2015 elections and in the subsequent negotiations. Since SYRIZA was a new party with few vested interests in the *status quo*, it was the party most likely to be able to bring about the fundamental socio-political changes that they themselves were advocating. But in the election campaign they refused to back it and after the elections they did everything possible to sabotage its efforts. The reason, of course, is that they themselves had vested interests in maintaining the *status quo*.

Tackling these problems is perhaps the biggest challenge facing the SYRIZA government. It recognises the need to do so and has the necessary political commitment. But, even with support from the 'Brussels Group', it will not be easy because the problems are deeply entrenched in the social and political culture. Moreover, they are the product of centuries of past history.

Unless or until SYRIZA succeeds in this mammoth task, there are two things that the outsider can do to beat the bureaucracy. The first, of course, is to learn Greek. The second is to do what the Cretans do – develop influential contacts and use them to one's advantage. The use of personal contacts actually has a number of advantages. I have gradually acquired a number of such contacts and I have found that it is not only an efficient way of doing business but also a pleasant one because one gets a personal service. For example, my accountant phoned me on a Saturday morning to ask me to come into his office to organise the payment of my property tax, and the insurance broker through whom I insure my property saw me walking past her office one morning and ran out into the street to tell me that my annual premium was due! In my view, this is far preferable to dealing with a computer or an automated phone line, as is now the case in most of the western world.

Attitudes and Behaviour of Outsiders

> It would appear that this is another case of intoxication
> and aggression involving tourists from Britain. It never
> happens with other nationals and it is very sad.
> (Manolis Michalodimitrakis, coroner, reported in *The
> Guardian*, 23 July 2014)

> But above all we have a foreign community that wants
> to integrate with local society. (Petarsis, M., *Festival
> of Culture*, Odysseus Program and Lyceum of Greek
> Women, Aghios Nikolaos, 2014)

The first of the above quotations relates to the stabbing by a
19-year-old British tourist of another British citizen during a
brawl outside a bar in Malia in July 2014. It is an extreme example, but unfortunately, as the quote suggests, such incidents are
not uncommon. Moreover, they are not the only way in which
outsiders' attitudes and behaviour hamper their relations with
the local population.

Part of the problem is simply one of cultural differences. Alcohol
is a case in point. Excessive alcoholic consumption is a problem
not only among tourists but also among some long-term residents, especially the British. In many towns and some villages,
one will find cafés where small groups of British expatriates congregate regularly. They spend a large part of the day there, and
drink continuously. Unlike the young tourists, these people can
hold their drink and so there are no problems of violence or ag-
gression. However, it must create a bad impression among the
local population. Greeks' attitude to alcohol is very different.
Although it is an essential part of their way of life, they seldom
drink to excess and alcoholism is relatively rare.

Another example is expatriates' attitudes towards animals. The
British in particular are renowned for their love of animals and
this has led to an interesting two-way movement of pets and pet

products between the UK and Crete. On the one hand, many British people bring their pets with them when they come to Crete. This applies not only to long-term residents, but also to some people coming for relatively short visits. I have met one couple who had come to Crete for four months and had brought their dog and another who were cruising the Mediterranean in a catamaran with their dog. Moreover, there is a surprising variety of pets. I know one family who brought their tortoises with them! Apparently, they had to certify that the tortoises had been born in the UK in order to get permission to bring them.

However, the British (and to a lesser extent other northern European nationals) are also concerned about the plight of animals in Crete, especially stray cats and dogs. There are several organisations that 'rescue' such animals and find homes for them in the UK or elsewhere and some individuals do the same. In the area where I live, one of the main 'problems' is, as I mentioned in Chapter 2, that of stray cats and a group of expatriates has established a charitable organisation that tries to address this issue. The organisation encourages people to bring cats to be neutered, a service for which it makes no charge, looks after those that are injured or ill, and finds homes for some in the UK. And sometimes it imports cat food from the UK (presumably because it is cheaper there than in Crete) to feed the cats in its care.

There is much controversy about this organisation within the local expatriate community. Many people think that their efforts are pointless, since they are only tackling the tip of the iceberg, and some argue that, by saving weak animals, they may actually be contributing to the problem. Some also fear that they may offend local people, because their efforts imply criticism of Cretan attitudes to animals. In its defence, the organisation claims that it has the support of the local council, which would like to control the population of feral animals but lacks the resources to do so. One cannot help wondering whether this is really a case of support, or merely toleration. However, whatever one's views about the organisation, one has to admire the sincerity of those involved and the amount of voluntary time and effort they devote to this cause.

Although differences in attitude to things like alcohol and animals can cause tensions, they are not, in my view, the main obstacle to integration. The main attitudinal problem is that many outsiders are not really concerned about integration. This is understandable, given their reasons for coming to Crete. For example, tourists come because it is a good place for a holiday, investors and economic migrants because of the economic opportunities, and retirees because they like the climate and relaxed way of life. Integration is thus not an aim in itself, but something pursued only when and to the extent necessary to achieve other objectives.

This is reflected in various ways. For example, as I have already indicated, many people do not make a serious attempt to learn Greek. They can get by in English (and, albeit to a lesser extent, some other languages), so there is no need to learn Greek. Another example is lack of interest in local politics and current events. I mentioned earlier that, in the run-up to the 2015 elections, I helped to organise a meeting with local SYRIZA representatives. However, very few people came and, both before and after these historic elections, I found few expatriates interested in discussing what was happening. Again, this is understandable. After all, there is not much that an expatriate can do to change the political situation. Moreover, their attitude towards politics is probably much the same in their home country – and many Greeks are equally disinterested in Greek politics.

However, the most obvious manifestation of this attitude to integration is the tendency for expatriates to mix with each other rather than with local people. This is of course inevitable in the case of tourists, but it is also prominent among long-term residents. It is reflected not just in their patterns of social behaviour, but also in a tendency to rely on fellow countrymen for professional or technical assistance, such as household renovations and maintenance, car repairs and even a haircut. And it is also reflected in the number of institutions established by the expatriate community to support their members. They range from commercial enterprises like the British Food Shop to social organisations, websites, newsletters and help lines. The British, perhaps because they are one of the largest expatriate communities, are an obvious example. But they are not the only one. Other Europeans are much the same, and so are the Pakistanis, the Chinese and the Africans.

This phenomenon is not unique to Crete. The Brits in Spain, the Asian and Polish communities in the UK and the whites in South Africa are only a few of the most obvious examples. Moreover, the Greeks tend to do the same when living in a foreign country. They have their own shops and churches and teach their children Greek. There are good reasons for this. People understandably feel more secure when dealing with people from their own culture. I will never forget the case of a Ugandan student whom I taught many years ago in the UK. Her husband was studying in Paris while she was in the UK and one day she heard that he was seriously ill and had been found to be HIV positive. Needless to say, she was distraught with worry, not only about him but also because of the risks to herself and their young daughter, who was with her in the UK. However, her concern about her husband was somewhat relieved when she learned that his friends had managed to find a Ugandan doctor in Paris to look after him.

Here in Crete, the language issue is part of the problem. It is easier to socialise with people who speak the same language, and if you are looking for someone to do some work on your house or your car, you need someone with whom you can communicate. I mentioned earlier the problem I had in communicating with my first electrician, who spoke very little English. But it is also a matter of trust. If you have a personal problem, you need someone in whom you can confide, and if you have a job to be done, you need someone on whom you can rely. And there is a tendency to trust people from one's own culture more than others, especially if, as is often the case in a relatively small expatriate community, you already know the person or they are recommended by someone whom you know. In my case, for example, the English builder who did most of the work on my apartment was recommended to me by my English neighbour. And, partly because he was a particularly good-natured person but also because of the cultural bond, he soon became someone whom I trusted and on whom I could rely.

This universal and understandable tendency for people to prefer to mix with their own kind is one of the main reasons why issues related to racial and cultural integration are not only sensitive but also highly complex. In multicultural societies, including the UK, there is much talk about the need for integration, but it is not something than can be forced. And this is true in Crete, as in the rest of the world.

However, this is only one side of the story. As the second of the two quotations at the beginning of this section suggests, many outsiders do want to integrate, and there are many efforts, by both individuals and organisations, to promote such integration. For example, in the area where I live there is an social organisation called the International Cultural Organisation of Aghios Nikolaos, otherwise known as INCO. It was established in 1998 'to represent the interests of all the foreign residents in the town and the surrounding villages'.[140] It organises a variety of social activities (including photography and gardening clubs and a walking group), helps any member with a personal problem (for example, someone who is hospitalised and has no-one to provide the personal care that in a Greek hospital is the responsibility of relatives or friends), acts as a general information service and, as and when necessary, liaises with local authorities on behalf of its members.

In some respects, INCO encourages separation rather than integration. For example, its membership is largely expatriate (Greeks can join but only as non-voting members) and most of the participants in its social activities are expatriates. However, one of its aims is to foster good relations with the local community and its leadership has made a special effort to do this. For example, it is represented on the board of a local charitable organisation that provides support for needy people in the area, raises funds for local causes (the Christmas 2014 raffle raised 3,600 euros to buy equipment for the hospital), and (as I have already noted) organised some meetings with local representatives of some of the political parties prior to the 2015 elections.

Moreover, INCO's efforts have been appreciated and in some cases reciprocated by local Cretan institutions. One such institution is the local branch of a women's organisation called the Lyceum of Greek Women (Λύκειο των Ελληνίδων). The Lyceum was established in 1911 - the same time as the Suffragettes reached the peak of their campaign in the UK – to promote the interests of Greek women. It has branches all over Greece and internationally. The Aghios Nikolaos branch appears to have three main objectives: the provision of opportunities for local women to learn skills and interact socially; the promotion of local culture and history; and the development of social and cultural relations with the town's expatriate community. In line with the third of these objectives, the local director, who is a particularly dynamic and energetic lady, has been keen to cooperate with INCO.

The cooperation between the two organisations goes back a number of years. However, it was strengthened in the winter of 2013-14, when some of the Greek classes organised under the *Odysseus* programme, which are attended by many INCO members, were held in the Lyceum's community centre. That was how I came to learn about the Lyceum. At the start of the classes, the director came to tell us about the organisation and its work and encouraged us to attend some of its social and cultural activities, which included the classes in traditional Cretan dancing that my friend Joan and I later joined. Although my dancing efforts did not last long, I attended other social events at the Lyceum and INCO began to use its community centre as a venue for its own activities.

In September 2014 the *Odysseus* programme and the Lyceum combined to organise a 'Festival of Culture', to which all INCO members were invited. The event included the presentation of certificates to those who had attended classes the previous winter, displays of traditional dancing and a 'pot-luck' meal, in which everyone brought some food traditional to their home country. The event was a great success. There were nearly a hundred people there, including the local mayor and bishop. At the time of writing, INCO and the Lyceum were discussing further ways of cooperating, including an art festival.

Conclusion

We have seen in this chapter that, for a variety of reasons, it is not easy for outsiders to become integrated into Cretan society. In fact, the attempts to foster integration described at the end of the last section, actually support this point. The existence of such activities is encouraging and they have helped me personally to feel at home in Aghios Nikolaos. However, their nature and, in particular, the mere fact that they are needed, reinforce my argument that integration is not easy. It is interesting, and perhaps significant, that the Greek word ξένος does not just mean 'foreigner'; it also means 'guest'. The Greek word for a hotel is ξενοδοκείο. Perhaps this helps to explain the Cretan attitude to outsiders; it is not just the tourists who are guests, we are all regarded as guests.

However, we have also seen that some people do become integrated, albeit to varying degrees. Those who speak Greek are more integrated than those who do not; second generation immigrants are more integrated than their parents; joining the Orthodox Church provides a gateway to participation in many other aspects of local society; and learning how to work the bureaucratic system makes life easier. Two main lessons emerge from this. Firstly, integration takes time. Secondly, and perhaps more significantly, those who integrate best are those who adopt the local language, religion and social culture. This is nothing new.

It was the same with the previous invasions. We saw in Chapter 3 that many previous invaders, from the early mainland Greeks to the Venetians and Turks, gradually, over several generations, became integrated into the local society and that, in order to do so, they had to adopt many local customs and norms. Those who did not remained merely guests.

EPILOGUE

Chapter 7

Uncaptured Crete: What Does the Future Hold?

'Crete,' I murmured. 'Crete ....' And my heart beat fast. (Kazantzakis, N., *Zorba the Greek*, London, Faber and Faber, 1961, p.34)

In Chapter 1, I explained that when I started writing this book I had two interrelated objectives: to explore the idea of an uncaptured Crete and to help clarify my own feelings about the island. In this final chapter, I will review my main findings and discuss the possible implications for the future – both for Crete and for me. The chapter is brief and my thoughts about the future of Crete purely speculative. Only time will tell.

Uncaptured Crete: For How Long?

In Part One of the book I described how, in the past, Crete was subject to countless invasions and occupations, but managed to maintain a sense of identity and spirit of independence, and I attributed this, at least in part, to its geography. In Part Two, I suggested that the island is currently in the midst of another invasion, fuelled by the dual processes of Europeanisation and globalisation, and I examined its impact on Cretan life and culture. I concluded that the concept of an uncaptured Crete appears still to be valid. Thanks to the combination of its geography and its history, the Cretans have remained as resilient as ever.

But one cannot help wondering how long this can last. The latest invasion is, in many respects, the most dangerous of all, because it is both subtle and all-pervasive. It is not something tangible, that one can fight against, and it is affecting all aspects of society – economic, political, social and cultural. In this respect, it perhaps resembles the period of Greek colonisation more than any of the later invasions and, as we have seen, that colonisation had an irrevocable effect on Crete.

The cultural effects are of particular concern. The generation gap in Crete at this point in time is vast. There are three, very different generations. First, there are the grandparents, who were born before 1974 and thus remember the turbulent times that preceded the restoration of democracy and the start of the present invasion. Then there are the parents, who were born and brought up in a democratic Greece and have learned how to survive the current invasion, with its booms and busts and dramatic technological changes. And then there are the youth, who have little direct knowledge of the past and are growing up in an exciting new digital, globalised world, but one in which their ambitions are frustrated by Greece's high rate of youth unemployment.

There is evidence of this generation gap everywhere. On the one hand, there are the bent old ladies, dressed in black, who make the sign of the cross every time they pass a church. On the other hand, there are the teenagers, whose lives, like those of teenagers throughout the western world, revolve around computers, mobile phones and the latest fashions in clothes or music. This juxtaposition of traditional and modern is, as I noted in Chapter 5, one of Crete's tourist attractions. However, it is also a threat to its society and, in particular, to the maintenance of its cultural identity. There are already some signs that things are changing, particularly but not only among the youth. Obese children and truculent teenagers, together with consumerism, online bullying and the breakdown of the extended family, are all becoming more common.

One of the most critical factors may be the future of the Greek language. We have seen in previous chapters that, in Crete as in Greece as a whole, language is of immense importance, not merely for its own sake but because it is inextricably linked with religion, culture and, in particular, a sense of identity and patriotism. At present, this association between language and identity is still very much alive. However, the globalisation of information, especially through the electronic media, presents an unprecedented threat to languages like Greek. I noted in Chapter 5 that the internet is the mode of communication in which English is most often used – and it is also the mode used most widely by the youth.

Another critical issue is the nature and extent of Crete's relationship with Greece. This is, of course, not a new issue. The relationship began in the period of Greek colonisation and its impact is reflected in all subsequent eras, most obviously in the debate over autonomy. At the end of Chapter 3, I expressed doubts about Detorakis' assumption that unification with Greece marked the end of Crete's history as an independent entity, and I think that the analysis in Part 2 has justified those doubts. Nevertheless, it is perhaps inevitable that, as time goes on, the differences between Crete and the rest of the country will become less.

However, when one looks back at Crete's long and complex history, these concerns seem less threatening. We have seen in this book that each of the previous invasions resulted in major societal changes, but not in a total loss of identity. The Cretan people were able to adopt some aspects of the invaders' society but reject others. In fact, this ability was one of the major reasons for their resilience. And we have seen that so far they seem to be adapting to the latest invasion in much the same way as in the past.

Moreover, a great deal will depend not on Crete's formal economic, political or cultural status, but on its image. The determining factor will be whether Cretans continue to regard themselves, and to be regarded by others, as an uncaptured people. This image may become more of a myth than a verifiable 'fact'. However, as I suggested in Chapter 3, the distinction between myth and reality is often blurred. Indeed, one could argue that the whole of my argument is based, at least in part, on myth. But if enough people continue to believe in the myth of an uncaptured Crete, it will continue to be as good as reality.

Furthermore, whatever happens to Cretan society, the island itself will endure and its physical environment will continue to limit the extent to which outsiders can gain control. In his novel *Freedom and Death*, which is set in Crete during the final years of Turkish occupation, one of the characters says: "Idiot, [Crete] won't be smashed, have no fear! We men are smashed, but not Crete, the immortal".[141]

Implications for Outsiders: What Does this Mean for Me?

How do I feel about Crete now? After writing this book, I have a better understanding not just of Crete but also of my feelings about living here. I now understand what it is about Crete that attracts me so much and what makes me feel slightly uneasy, and I understand why I feel so much at home and yet still feel like an 'outsider'.

So what will I do? Will I stay in Crete, and if so how will I adapt, or will I leave? I have actually decided to leave. However, the reasons for this decision have more to do with me than with Crete. There are only two reasons related to Crete. One is the wind, which I find very wearing. It epitomises for me the harsh side of the island's physical environment. The other, and much more important, reason is the language barrier. I have accepted that, if I were to stay, I would always be an outsider – or, to put it more positively, a guest. But that it is not what concerns me. I am used to living in other countries and being a guest. However,

I like to be able to follow what is going on around me and to be able to participate in some way or other, and that is very difficult with only a rudimentary knowledge of Greek. If I was younger, it might be different. I would have the time and hopefully also the mental ability to become more fluent.

The main reason for my decision to leave stems from my own personality. Like Zorba (and Kazantzakis himself), I am a restless person, always wanting to see new places and find out how other people live, and always in search of greener pastures. Consequently, I seldom stay in one place for more than a few years and the time has come when I feel the need to move on again.

But I have no regrets whatsoever about coming to Crete. It has been a fascinating experience - one that I would recommend to anyone. Moreover, I will miss the island. I will miss the landscape, especially the juxtaposition of sea and mountains and the magnificent views. I will miss the long, hot summers, when I am able to live out-of-doors. I will miss my early morning swims and my winter walks in the hills. I will miss my local landmarks, Thilakas and the Cha Gorge, and most of all, my local Almyros beach. I will miss the street-café culture and the traditional village *tavernas*. I will miss the fresh fruit and vegetables and the pleasure of picking oranges and lemons from my own trees. I will even miss my struggles with the Greek language and bureaucracy. And I will miss the resilience of the Cretan people. Like Kazantzakis, whenever I think of Crete, my heart will beat fast.

Select Bibliography

Andriotis, K., 'Local authorities in Crete and the development of tourism,' *Journal of Tourism Studies* 13(2003): 53-62.

Andriotis, K. and R.D. Vaughan, 'Urban residents' attitudes toward tourism development: the case of Crete', *Journal of Travel Research* 42 (2003): 172-85.

Atlas of Crete (The), Athens: Anavasi Digital, 2010.

Detorakis T., *History of Crete*, Second edition, Heraklion, 1994. This is the English translation of a Greek text. The book has been republished several times. The latest edition was published in Iraklio by Mystis Editions in 2015.

Economides, I., *The Two Faces of Greece*, Athens, 1992.

Hislop, V., *The Island*. Headline Review, 2005.

Humphrys, J., *Blue Skies and Black Olives*, Hodder and Stoughton, 2009.

Hyden, G., *Beyond Ujamaa in Tanzania: Underdevelopment and an Uncaptured Peasantry*, Heinemann, 1980.

International Labour Organisation (ILO), *World Social Protection Report 2014/15*. Geneva, 2014.

Kazantzakis, N., *Zorba the Greek*, London, Faber and Faber, 1961.

Kazantzakis, N., *Freedom and Death*, London, Faber and Faber, 1966.

Leontitsis, Vasileios, *Decentralisation Reforms in Greece (1981-2008)*, Ph.D. thesis, University of Sheffield, 2009.

Llewellyn Smith, M., *Crete: The Great Island*, online edition, Sunshade Press, 2007, p.158; originally published by Longmans in 1965.

Lopes, C., 'Structural adjustment policies and Africa: a reply to Shantayanan Devararajan,' *Think Africa Press* (http://thinkafricapress.com), 25 November 2013.

Makrakis, M., *Elounda, Agios Nikolaos,Spinalonga: Their History*, Smerniotakis Publishing, English translation; n.d(probably about 2010).

McGuire, G., *Minoan Intrusions*, Archaeolomultimedia Publishing, 2014.

Moorey, C., *A Glimpse of Heaven: Introduction to Greek Orthodox Churches and Worship for Visitors*, Athens, Efstathiadis Group, 2004 (also available as Kindle book).

Nicolson, A., *The Mighty Dead: Why Homer Matters*, London, William Collins, 2014.

Oxfam, *The True Cost of Austerity and Inequality in Europe. Greece Case Study.* 2013.

Panagiotakis, G., *The Epic Battle of Crete,* Iraklio, 2012.

Rackham, O. and J. Moody, *The Making of the Cretan Landscape*, Manchester University Press, 1996.

Rosen, T., 'The Chinese-ification of Greece', *Cultural Anthropology Online*, 30 October 2011.

Sfikas, G., *Birds and Mammals of Crete*, Athens: Efstathiadis Group, 2006.

Vasilakis, A.S., *The Great Inscription of the Law Code of Gortyn*, Iraklio, Mystis Editions, no date.

Notes

Chapter 1

1 Llewellyn Smith, M., *Crete: The Great Island,* online edition, Sunshade Press, 2007, p.158; originally published by Longmans in 1965.

2 The book was published by Heinemann in 1980.

Chapter 2

3 Rackham, O. and J, Moody, *The Making of the Cretan Landscape,* Manchester University Press, 1996, p.13.

4 Cross, T., *A Study of the Geological Setting of Lake Voulismeni in Agios Nikolaos, Crete,* unpublished manuscript, 2014.

5 Rackham and Moody, 1996, p.12.

6 The Greek letter χ, which is usually transliterated as *ch* is pronounced like the *ch* in 'loch', so Cha is pronounced more like *Ha*. The same applies with the name of Crete's second largest town, Chania, which is pronounced more like *Hania*.

7 Rackham and Moody, 1996, p.213.

8 Cross, T., 2014; Makrakis, M., *Elounda, Spinalonga, Agios Nikolaos: Their History.* Smirniotakis Publishing, n.d., p.174.

9 *Greek Reporter* (online newspaper) (http://greece.greekreporter.com), 19 May 2015.

10 Rackham and Moody, 1996, pp.33-34.

11 Rackham and Moody, 1996, p.37.

12 *The Atlas of Crete,* Athens: Anavasi Digital, 2010, p.14.

13 *The Atlas of Crete,* 2010, p.12.

14 Rackham and Moody, 1996, p.82.

15 Rackham and Moody, 1996, p.80-81.

16 Rackham and Moody, 1996, p.112.

17 Rackham and Moody, 1996, p.63.

18 Rackham and Moody, 1996, p.57.

19 Rackham and Moody, 1996, p.47.

20 Rackham and Moody, 1996, p.46.

21 Sfikas, G., *Birds and Mammals of Crete*, Athens: Efstathi-adis Group, 2006.

22 http://avibase.bsc-eoc.org/checklist.jsp?region=GRcr

23 http://www.crete-guide.info/snakes_crete.htm

Chapter 3

24 Detorakis, T., *History of Crete*, Second edition, Herak-lion, 1994. This is the English translation of a Greek text. The book has been republished several times. The latest edition was published in Iraklio by Mystis Editions in 2015.

25 Llewellyn Smith, M., *Crete: the Great Island*. Longman, 1965. This book is out-of-print, but an online edition, which can be downloaded free, was published by Sunshade Press in 2007. References here are to the online edition.

26 Makrakis, M., *Elounda, Agios Nikolaos,Spinalonga: Their History*, Smerniotakis Publishing, English translation;, n.d,,(probably about 2010).

27 The research was undertaken by the Plakias Stone Age Project, a collaborative US-Greek project (see http://pla-kiasstoneageproject.com)

28 Beckmann, S., *Domesticating Mountains in Middle Bronze Age Crete: Minoan Agricultural Landscaping in the Aghios Nikolaos Region*. Rethymno, Department of History and Archaeology, University of Crete, Doctoral thesis, 2012.

29 This information is based on an article published in a journal called *Nature Communications*, which was reported by the BBC on 15 May 2013 (http://www.bbc.com/news/science-environ-ment-22527821).

30 Rackham, O. and J. Moody, *The Making of the Cretan Landscape*, Manchester University Press, 1996, p.1.

31 This is derived from a chart in Wikipedia (http://ancient-greece.org/resources/timeline.html)

32 For an interesting discussion on the origin and inter-pretation of Homer's works, see Adam Nicolson's book, *The Mighty Dead: Why Homer Matters* (London, William Collins, 2014).

33 Rackham and Moody, 1996, p.2.

34 Detorakis,1994, p.40.

35 Mary Renault, *Fire from Heaven* (1969); *The Persian Boy* (1972); *Funeral Games* (1981). All are published by Pantheon Books.

36 Rackham and Moody,1996, p.94.

37 Detorakis, 1994, pp.52-53.

38 Makrakis, n.d,, p.25.

39 For a detailed account of this code of law and the Gortyn archaeological site, see Vasilakis, A.S., *The Great Inscription of the Law Code of Gortyn*, Iraklio, Mystis Editions, no date.

40 Detorakis, 1994, p.45.

41 Detorakis, 1994, pp.68-80. See also Cummings, E., 'Pirates and merchants: evidence for a thriving Hellenic Crete', *2015 AIA/SCS Joint Annual Meeting*, New Orleans, January 2015. This paper was based on an undergraduate honors thesis (*Crete in the Hellenistic Aegean: Seeing Through the Cretan Mirage*. University of Colorado, Spring 2014), which is available on the internet.

42 Rackham and Moody, p.2. Detorakis (1996, pp.98-103) lists and maps 144 'cities' that existed at some time between the Minoan and Roman times.

43 Makrakis, n.d,, p.44.

44 Makrakis, n.d., p.34.

45 It appears that Marcus Antonius was also given the name 'Creticus', but in this case it was a sign of shame rather than honour.

46 Makrakis, n.d,, p.27.

47 Detorakis,1994, pp.88-89.

48 Llewellyn Smith, 2007, p.21.

49 Detorakis, 1994, p.106.

50 Llewellyn Smith, 2007, p.17. Most of the information in this paragraph is derived from this source.

51 Economides, I., *The Two Faces of Greece*, Athens, 1992, pp.77, 80. Economides' views should be treated with caution, since her works are very biased in favour of Greek people, Greek culture and, in particular, the Orthodox Church. However, these quotations give a good impression of the esteem with

which Byzantine culture is regarded in Greece.

52 Detorakis, 1994, pp.109-14.

53 These comments are based on my reading of three writers: Detorakis, Makrakis and Llewellyn Smith. Makrakis presents the first view and Llewellyn Smith the second, while Detorakis presents both perspectives.

54 Detorakis,1994, p.135.

55 Makrakis, n.d,, pp.54-56.

56 Detorakis, 1994, p.123.

57 Detorakis, 1994, p.123.

58 Detorakis, 1994, p.144. This summary of events is based primarily but not entirely on this source. When I read about the sale of Crete I was reminded of what I thought was the historical fact that Queen Victoria gave Mount Kilimanjaro to Kaiser Wilhelm because she had two mountains in East Africa and he had none. But when I checked this on the internet, I found that this was another myth!

59 Llewellyn Smith, 2007, p.50.

60 Llewellyn Smith, 2007, p.51.

61 Detorakis, 1994, p.191.

62 Rackham and Moody,1996, p.95.

63 Detorakis, 1994, p.153.

64 Makrakis, n.d,, p.16.

65 Makrakis, n.d., p.61.

66 Makrakis, n.d., p.64.

67 Detorakis, 1994, pp.251, 271.

68 Llewellyn Smith, 2007, chapter 7; Rackham and Moody, 1996, p.4.

69 Ministry of Culture and Tourism, *Spinalonga,* information leaflet, 2011.

70 Detorakis, 1994, p.261.

71 Rackham and Moody, 1996, p.4.

72 Rackham and Moody, 1996, p.4.

73 Detorakis, 1994, pp.379-80.

74 Detorakis, 1994, p.340.

75 Detorakis, 1994, p. 319.

76 Detorakis, 1994, pp.347-50.

77 Kazantzakis, N., *Freedom and Death*, London, Faber and Faber, 1966 (original Greek edition 1953).

78 Detorakis, 1994, p.406.

79 These figures are from *Wikipedia*. Interestingly, Detorakis makes no mention of this election, only of the subsequent vote in the Assembly.

80 Llewellyn Smith, 2007, p.100.

81 Detorakis, 1994, p.430.

82 Makrakis, n.d., p.108.

83 Most of those written in English are by British authors, in some cases people who were actually involved in the confrontation. However, in 2012 a Greek writer, George Panagiotakis, published a book about the battle, written in four languages - Greek, English, German and Russian. The English title is *The Epic Battle of Crete*. The book presents a Greek perspective and includes an excellent collection of photographs.

84 Panagiotakis, 2012.

85 Rackham and Moody, 1996, p.99.

86 Llewellyn Smith, 2007, pp.3-4.

87 Rackham and Moody, 1996, p.99.

88 Makrakis, n.d., p.20. Most of the information in the this paragraph is taken from Makrakis' book.

89 The union between Scotland and England was not fully legalised until 1707, but they were effectively united in 1603, when King James VI of Scotland became King James I of England. In the 2014 referendum, 45% of the population voted for independence and 55% against.

Chapter 4

90 The song was part of a 1971 album called 'Blue'.

91 Andriotis, K. and R.D. Vaughan, 'Urban residents' attitudes toward tourism development: the case of Crete', *Journal of Travel Research* 42 (2003): 172-85; Andriotis, K., 'Local authorities in Crete and the development of tourism,' *Journal of Tourism Studies* 13(2003): 53-62; 'In focus: Crete, Greece', *4Hoteliers: Hotel, Travel and Hospitality News*, 11 February 2014 (www.4hoteliers.

com); *Sfakia-Crete-Forum.com* (www.sfakia-crete.com)11 November 2014.

92 Association of Greek Tourism Enterprises, *Greek Tourism Facts and Figures* (online publication).

93 *Greek Reporter* (online newspaper) (http://greece.greekreporter.com), 28 March 2015.

94 In 2008 (the most recent year for which I have been able to find data, it accounted for 40% of national income and 36% of employment (Hersonissos Tourist Guide 2014; www.hersonisos.com).

95 Andriotis, K. and R.D. Vaughan, 'Urban residents' attitudes toward tourism development: the case of Crete', *Journal of Travel Research* 42 (2003): 172-85.

96 www.investingreece.gov.gr.

97 *Ekathimerini.com* (English edition of Greek online newspaper) (http://www.ekathimerini.com), 26 November 2014.

98 Rosen, T., 'The Chinese-ification of Greece', *Cultural Anthropology Online*, 30 October 2011.

99 *Greek Reporter*, 7 October 2014.

100 *Ekathimerini.com*,15 and 24 November 2014, 27 April 2015.

101McGuire, G., *Minoan Intrusions*, Archaeolomultimedia Publishing, 2014.

102 *Ekathimerini.com*, 31 March 2015.

103 *Ekathimerini.com*, 10 December 2014; Reuters (uk.reuters.com), 7 May 2015.

104 BBC News online, 5 May 2015.

105 For details of these reforms, see Vasileios Leontitsis, *Decentralisation Reforms in Greece (1981-2008)*, Ph.D. thesis, University of Sheffield, 2009.

106 *Greek Reporter*, 22 May 2015.

107 *Ekathimerini.com*, 13 August 2014.

108 For a recent critique, see Lopes, C., 'Structural adjustment policies and Africa: a reply to Shantayanan Devararajan,' *Think Africa Press* (http://thinkafricapress.com), 25 November 2013.

109 *Ekathimerini.com*, 30 June 2014.

110 International Labour Organisation (ILO), *World Social*

Protection Report 2014/15. Geneva, 2014
   111 *Greek Reporter*, 22 May 2015.
   112 *Ekathimerini.com*, 12 December 2014.
   113 *Greek Reporter*, 25 May 2015.
   114 International Labour Organisation (ILO), *World Social Protection Report 2014/15.* Geneva, 2014; Oxfam, *The True Cost of Austerity and Inequality in Europe. Greece Case Study.* 2013.

Chapter 5

   115 Hislop, V., *The Island.* Headline Review, 2005.
   116 Hersonissos Tourist Guide 2014, (www.hersonisos.com)
   117 'Olive growers' claims prompt investigation', *New York Times* 27 December 2009. 'EU funds for projects that never existed', Deutsche Welle, *Top Stories*, 20 July 2012. Both reports accessed online 7 January 2015. .
   118 BBC News, 15 November 2004. Downloaded from the internet on 19 August 2014.
   119 www.crete.org.uk/cretan-laguage
   120 The findings of this survey were reported in *Wikipedia*.
   121 *Eurobarometer Special Report 415*. The respondents were actually asked 'Which are the most important values for you: tolerance, religion, self-fulfilment, respect for other cultures, or other?'
   122 http://hdr.undp.org/en/content/table-4-gender-inequality-index
   123 *Ekathimerini.com*,15 and 20 June 2014.
   124 www.greece.greekreporter.com, 14 May 2015. LGBTI is an acronym for lesbian, gay, bisexual, transsexual and intersexual.
   125 Llewellyn Smith, M., *Crete: The Great Island*, online edition, Sunshade Press, 2007, p.173.
   126 One could argue that this is another example of Greeks' negative view of the Turkish era, since, as we saw in Chapter 3, the Romans, Byzantines and, in particular, the Venetians also imposed heavy taxation.
   127 *Ekathimerini.com*, 9 September 2014.

Chapter 6

128 Rackham, O. and J, Moody, *The Making of the Cretan Landscape*, Manchester University Press, 1996, p.36.

129 Rackham and Moody, 1996, p.36.

130 Rackham and Moody, 1996, p.93.

131 Rackham and Moody, 1996, p.36.

132 Hislop, V., *The Island*. Headline Review, 2005.

133 The Greek word for tongue, γλώσσα (pronounced 'glossa'), also means language.

134 http://ekathimerini.com and http://greece.greekreporter.com

135 Information provided at a 'Festival of Culture', organised jointly by the Odysseus programme and the Lyceum of Greek Women, in Aghios Nikolaos in September 2014.

136 Humphrys, John, *Blue Skies and Black Olives*, Hodder and Stoughton, 2009.

137 It appears that in Ancient Greek and Latin, punctuation consisted of various kinds of dots. The length and type of pause was indicated by the number of dots and their position (level with the bottom, middle or top of the preceding letters). Full stops, colons and semi-colons are relics of this system. Apparently, the original Greek question mark was not exactly the same as a semi-colon; however, it was similar and so over time the semi-colon was adopted.

138 Boukalas, P., 'National self-awareness put to the test', *ekathimerini.com*, 21 May 2015.

139 Moorey, C., *A Glimpse of Heaven: Introduction to Greek Orthodox Churches and Worship for Visitors* (2004); *Travelling Companions: Walking with the Saints of the Church* (2013); *Crowns of Barbed Wire: Orthodox Christian Martyrs of the 20th Century* (2015).

140 www.inconews.com

Chapter 7

141 Kazantzakis, N., *Freedom and Death*, London, Faber and Faber, 1966, p.74.

1.Thilakas, with Dhikti Mountains in background

2. Cha Gorge

3.Almyros beach in winter

4.Reed-beds at Almyros

5.Lasithi Plateau

6.Gournia, site of Minoan town

7.Spinalonga island

8.Aghios Nikolas, with Lake Voulismeni in foreground

9.Easter Saturday night celebration, Aghios Nikolaos

10.Kafeneio Michalis Skoulas, Anogeia

11.Musicians, Platanos taverna, Myrtos

12.Crete's generation gap